PHILIPPIANS

PHILIPPIANS

$\blacklozenge$

H. A. IRONSIDE

Revised Edition

Introductory Notes by
John Phillips

LOIZEAUX
Neptune, New Jersey

First Edition, 1922
Revised Edition, 1996

PHILIPPIANS
© 1996 by Loizeaux Brothers, Inc.

A Publication of Loizeaux Brothers, Inc.
*A Nonprofit Organization Devoted to the Lord's Work
and to the Spread of His Truth*

Unless otherwise indicated, Scripture quotations are taken from the
King James version of the Bible.

Profile taken from *Exploring the Scriptures*
© 1965, 1970, 1989 by John Phillips

Library of Congress Cataloging-in-Publication Data

Ironside, H. A. (Henry Allan), 1876-1951.
Philippians / H.A. Ironside. — Rev. ed. / introductory notes
by John Phillips.
Rev. ed. of: Philippians, Colossians, Thessalonians. 1st ed. 1922.
ISBN 0-87213-413-X (pbk.: alk. paper)
1. Bible. N.T. Philippians—Commentaries. I. Ironside, H. A.
(Henry Allan), 1876-1951. Philippians, Colossians, Thessalonians.
II. Title.
BS2705.3.I76   1996
227'.6077—dc20   96-44163

Printed in the United States of America
10 9 8 7 6 5 4 3 2 1

CONTENTS

A PROFILE
PHILIPPIANS
CONTINUAL REJOICING

BY JOHN PHILLIPS

Paul's letter to the Philippians was sent to the first Christian church he planted in Europe. His first visit to their city was on his second missionary journey and he was accompanied by Silas, Timothy, and probably Luke (Acts 16).

The city of Philippi, a Roman military colony in Macedonia, probably had very few Jews in its population. Persecution of the missionaries at Philippi had arisen from Gentile sources. Only twice in the book of Acts is Gentile hostility thus expressed and on each occasion the gospel had threatened vested financial interests.

The Philippian believers had retained their first love for Paul and had helped him more than once with his financial needs. The apostle showed his gratitude repeatedly in the Epistle.

The church at Philippi was free of the many errors that called forth most of Paul's other letters. The apostle's reasons for writing to the Philippians were twofold: he wished to acknowledge receipt of the financial gift delivered by Epaphroditus; and he wished to urge some of the members of the church to lay aside animosity and live in peace with one another.

Written in prison by a man chained day and night to a soldier, this letter nevertheless resounds with a note of joy. The author had few friends in Rome and numerous vocal enemies, yet the word *rejoice* and its synonyms occur sixteen times in four short chapters.

The structure of the book of Philippians can be defined in terms of Paul's experiences, examples, and exhortations:

Paul's Triumphant Experiences

Satan might keep a man like Paul from traveling, but he can never keep him from triumphing. The Epistle to the Philippians illustrates the phrase "more than conquerors" (Romans 8:37).

There was one man in the Philippian church who knew that Paul's emphasis on joy was real. That man was the jailer who had learned that neither chastisement nor chains could blunt the edge of Paul's triumph in Christ. This jailer dated his conversion from the night that Paul and Silas had sung the songs of Zion in the Philippian jail until the very foundations of the prison had rocked.

The Epistle to the Philippians gives us the key to the triumphant joy that laughs at tribulation: "For to me to live is Christ," Paul said, "and to die is gain" (Philippians 1:21). This outlook on life transformed misery into melody, prisons into palaces, and Roman soldiers into souls to be won for Christ. The first chapter of Philippians throbs with this triumph. "My bonds!" exclaimed Paul again and again. He said in effect, "Thank God for these bonds! Through them the entire praetorian guard has been told of a greater king than Nero. Through these bonds many have taken courage to be bold for Christ. Yes, these bonds have taught me to prize my prospects of an abundant entrance into the Savior's presence."

Paul's Tremendous Examples

Paul's triumphs can be shared by all because of the triumph of Christ. Paul bade the saints to arm themselves with the mind of Christ and manifest the true Christian spirit. Paul wanted his readers to consider the example of our Lord, who laid aside His glory and stooped to conquer. Christ did not think that equality with God was a thing to be grasped, yet He clothed Himself with humanity, "humbled himself, and became obedient unto death, even the death of the cross" (Philippians 2:8). And from this great stoop He was exalted on high and given the supreme name. Are not the implications clear for all Christians? Those who follow in His steps will experience a transformation of conduct, character, and concept.

Paul also cited the examples of Timothy and Epaphroditus, who became "more than conquerors" in service and in sickness. The apostle reminded the Philippians that Timothy's service was characterized by a true, total, and tested commitment to Christ. Then Paul wrote about how the sickness of Epaphroditus had affected him as well as the patient and how it should affect the Philippians.

Paul's Typical Exhortations

In the last two chapters Paul made some practical applications. We need a proper theology of Christ if we are to experience His triumph. "That I may win Christ," said Paul in Philippians 3:8, bringing into focus the truth of reward. "That I may know him," he said in 3:10, underlining the truth of sanctification. "That I may apprehend," he said in 3:12, emphasizing the truth of service.

Paul showed how positive thinking has its place in the life of a child of God. After all, we can only think of one thing at a time. If the mind is occupied with things that are true, honest, just, pure, and lovely—things of good report—then virtue and praise will flow from the life.

Paul did not forget that the praising man is the prevailing man, for he closed the Epistle on a note of thanksgiving, contentment, and praise. The man who has learned how to interpret the circumstances of life in the light of Calvary can thank God, come what may. Paul could say, "I have learned, in whatsoever state I am, therewith to be content....I can do all things through Christ which strengtheneth me" (Philippians 4:11-13). Those who have learned the secret of contentment will not react negatively to adverse situations; they will act triumphantly. They will be "more than conquerors."

PREFATORY NOTE

TO FIRST EDITION

These notes have been jotted down at odd times over a period of nearly two years while the writer has been busily engaged in gospel work. They pretend to no literary value and repetitions may sometimes occur, but the notes, such as they are, are sent forth with the earnest hope that they may be blessed to some of the "quiet in the land" (Psalm 35:20) who enjoy simple things plainly put.

H. A. Ironside
July 1922

INTRODUCTION

The account of the labors and sufferings of the apostle Paul and his companions in Philippi is given in Acts 16. They went to Macedonia in response to a vision Paul had seen at Troas: a vision of a man of that country calling for help. But apparently when they reached the capital, no such man was waiting for them. Instead they came in touch with a few women who were accustomed to gather for prayer in a quiet place by the riverside outside the city. There the Lord opened Lydia's heart to listen to the words of Paul. Others also were reached, among them some brethren (Acts 16:40). But it was when Paul was cast into prison that the greatest work was done. The jailer and his household were won for Christ before the messengers of God's grace departed for Thessalonica.

The infant church was very dear to the heart of the apostle, and he was very dear to the Philippian believers. After he left them, they showed their love and care at various times and probably for a number of years. But at last they lost touch with him, apparently during his imprisonment at Caesarea. When he was in Rome they again communicated with him. Fearing he might be in need, they sent him an expression of their love with a trusted and beloved brother named Epaphroditus. Having fulfilled his ministry, this faithful man became sick, and his illness was of sufficient duration for word of it to reach Philippi and cause anxiety among the saints there. News of their concern reached Rome about the time that Epaphroditus became convalescent. He decided to return at once, and Paul entrusted him with his letter to the Philippians. Apparently the letter was dictated to him by the apostle.

The book of Philippians is an epistle of joy, a letter of cheer. It also contains needed exhortation for a wilderness people, liable to

13

fall by the way. Epaphroditus, it seems, had communicated to Paul a concern that was weighing on his heart regarding a misunderstanding or quarrel between two women in Philippi, both of whom were much esteemed by the saints there and by the apostle himself. If the squabble was not checked and healed, it was likely to prove a source of sadness and possibly even division in the church in days to come.

With this misunderstanding evidently much on his mind as he wrote, the apostle sought to present Christ so that the hearts of all would be enraptured with Him, all selfish aims would disappear, and all that was of the flesh would be judged in His presence. The message of the book of Philippians is needed whenever the flesh is at work among believers. That is why this portion of the Word of God has such importance in the present hour of the church's history.

The theme of the Epistle can be expressed in the three words, "Christ is all" (Colossians 3:11). Philippians is the Epistle of Christ; it occupies us with Himself. The book falls naturally into four divisions, which are indicated by the four chapters, and each division presents Christ in a different way. Each chapter also indicates the results that should be seen in the lives of believers as they meditate on the aspect of Christ presented in that particular passage.

Chapter 1 sets forth Christ as our life—and the evangelistic spirit or gospel mind that believers should cultivate.

Chapter 2 sets forth Christ as our example—and the lowly mind or humble spirit of those who follow Him.

Chapter 3 sets forth Christ as our object—and the steadfast spirit or determined mind of those whose hearts and thoughts are centered on Himself.

Chapter 4 sets forth Christ as our strength and supply—and the confident mind or spirit of trust that should characterize all who know the resources that are in Him.

This Epistle is practical. It has to do with our state rather than our standing, with responsibility rather than privilege, with communion rather than union. In other words, this Epistle is suited to our wilderness journey, written to guide our feet while going through this world. Paul's letter to the Philippians is a pastoral ministry of a very precious kind.

Others have written fully and helpfully on this part of the Word of God. It is not my intention to attempt a labored exposition of the Epistle, but simply to jot down some notes that embody the results of my own study. My hope is that these notes may be used by the Holy Spirit for the edification and comfort of fellow saints, particularly those who are discouraged. I have gleaned much from what others have taught and I make no pretension of originality. If Christ Himself becomes a little more appreciated by a few of His own, I will have accomplished my goal.

CHAPTER ONE
CHRIST, THE BELIEVER'S LIFE

Salutation (Philippians 1:1-2)

In many of his letters Paul linked himself with younger and less experienced fellow-laborers, as in his greeting here. An apostle by the Lord's call, Paul occupied a unique place as His special messenger to the Gentiles. But he never stood aloof in complacent dignity, apart from others who were engaged in the same ministry. He had taken Timothy with him when the young man had not been a believer for long, and later in this letter Paul testified of the truth that was in Timothy.

In his care for the development of the younger brethren, Paul became a model for older teachers and evangelists throughout the dispensation. If others are to follow in the ministry, more experienced men must take personal interest in less experienced brothers who show promise. By associating with young believers in ministry, the older men can lead and encourage them in the path of faith. It is often the other way, and the young become disheartened and slip back into worldly pursuits. If they had been wisely advised and helped when needed, they might have become able ministers of the truth.

Paul and Timothy took no official title in Philippians 1:1. They simply called themselves "servants of Jesus Christ." The word translated "servants" here means "bondmen." Paul and Timothy were purchased servants and as such belonged entirely to Him whom they gladly owned as their anointed Master. They were His and renounced all rights to do the will of the flesh.

17

It is not only ministering brethren who are designated "servants of Jesus Christ" in Scripture. This name is used of all Christians. Though sons and heirs, we are also bondmen of love, whose delight it should be to yield ourselves to Him, as befitting those who are alive from the dead.

Paul greeted the saints at Philippi and made special mention of the elders and deacons. This special mention is unusual. It implies a particular sense of obligation to the elders and deacons, probably in connection with their church's gift of love. The apostle may also have thought of addressing the leaders or guides in a special way in view of the unhappiness between Euodias and Syntyche, which he wished to rectify.

Elders may or may not be official. In the early church they were definitely appointed by apostolic authority. Today it may be unwise, and going beyond Scripture, for saints without that apostolic authority to set up or ordain official elders. On the other hand, those obviously possessing the qualifications indicated in the Epistles to Timothy and Titus should be recognized by fellow believers as God-appointed elders, whose counsel should be sought and whose responsibility it is to watch over souls and oversee the house of God. To fail to recognize such qualified men would be lack of subjection to the Word of God. A true bishop or overseer would be the last man to insist on obedience to him. He would rather lead by serving the saints and by the force of a godly example.

Deacons, who minister in temporal things, should be chosen by the saints for this purpose. The word *deacon* means "servant," not in the sense of "bondman," but in the sense of one who acts voluntarily and in response to the expressed desire of others.

Notice the little word "all" in Philippians 1:1. It is used in a significant way in this Epistle and is not used in the same way anywhere else in the writings of the apostle. Observe the use of the word in 1:1,4,7,8,25 and 2:26. It is plain that Paul desired to bind all the Philippian believers together in one bundle of love, refusing even to seem to recognize any incipient division among them. He greeted them *all;* he thought well of them *all;* he prayed for them *all.* He knew that in the end it would be well with them *all,* so he exhorted them *all* to stand fast in one spirit.

As was customary in his letters, Paul wished his friends grace and peace, linking the two blessings together. "Grace" was the usual Grecian salutation. "Peace" was that of the Hebrew. Grace in its highest sense—undeserved favor—can only be known by the Christian. True peace—whether peace *with* God, which is fundamental, or the peace *of* God—rests on the work of the cross. The apostle's wish for the saints at Philippi was that they would enter into and enjoy the peace of God from day to day. Both kinds of peace come from God the Father and from our Lord Jesus Christ, through whom we have been brought into this place of favor.

Introduction (Philippians 1:3-11)

In these verses we have the apostle's own introduction to this delightful specimen of early Christian correspondence. His interest in the saints at Philippi had not ceased with his leaving their city. Through the passing years he had kept them in his heart and presented them to God in prayer. There were sweet and blessed memories too that filled him with gladness as he looked back on the time of ministry spent among them and as he learned of their continuing in the grace of God.

Paul thanked God for every remembrance of them. There was nothing, apparently, in their past history that caused him pain or anxiety of mind. And so, in every prayer of his for them all, he made his requests with joy. Their fellowship with him in the gospel had been consistent from the beginning. Notice the significance the word "fellowship" has in this Epistle and how frequently "the gospel" is mentioned. An assembly of saints walking together in the fear of the Lord, exercised about presenting the word of life to the unsaved, is likely to know more of real fellowship than a company of believers occupied chiefly with their own affairs and blessings. On the other hand, no assembly can prosper that fails to recognize the importance of the divine and holy principles given in the Word to guide believers while they are in this world.

"Fellowship in the gospel" (Philippians 1:5) may be experienced in various ways: by prayer, by participation in public testimony, and by furnishing the means that enable laborers to carry on the

Lord's work unhindered by anxiety. All servants of Christ going forth for His name's sake, "taking nothing of the Gentiles" (3 John 7), should be entirely cast on the Lord for His support. On the other hand, it should be esteemed a privilege by those remaining at home to help those laborers by ministering in temporal things. Such ministry will never be forgotten by Him who said, "He that receiveth a prophet in the name of a prophet shall receive a prophet's reward" (Matthew 10:41).

I remember another believer's definition of *fellowship*. He was a teamster. When he was asked, "What do you understand by *fellowship?*" he replied, "For each one to pull his own trace and keep it tight."

The apostle had no doubt as to the final outcome for every true believer. He was absolutely confident that the One who had begun a good work in them would not stop until He had perfected that which He Himself had commenced. But the final outcome would only be attained and manifested in the day of Jesus Christ. A godly old brother used to say, "The Lord always looks at His people as they will be when they are done." It would be good for us to learn to look at them in the same way.

An incident is told of an artist who had conceived in his mind a great picture that he meant to be the masterpiece of his life. He was working on a large canvas, putting in the drabs and grays that were to compose the background, when a friend entered unnoticed. The artist worked on with enthusiasm, not aware of the onlooker's presence. Finally, happening to turn, the artist saw him and exclaimed, "What do you think of this? I intend it to be the greatest work I have ever done."

His friend burst into laughter and replied, "Why, to be frank, I don't think much of it. It seems to me to be only a great daub."

"Ah," replied the artist, at once sensing the situation, "you cannot see what is going to be there. I can."

So it is with God our Father. He sees in every believer that which will be fully brought out at the judgment seat of Christ, and He is working now toward that end. We too often see the present imperfection and forget the future glory. But in the day of Jesus Christ when all shall be manifested, every believer will be conformed to the image of God's blessed Son. Surely we can join with the apostle even now and say, "It is meet for me to think this of you all" (Philippians 1:7). To look on God's people in this manner will deliver us from much strife and disappointment when we see carnality in those from whom we expected better things. It is humbling and helpful to remember that others probably see similar imperfections in us.

Paul carried the saints at Philippi in his heart. Though in prison, he recognized their fellowship in the defense and confirmation of the gospel and he rejoiced in the manner in which they shared this grace with him. He called God to witness how greatly he yearned after every one of them in the tender love of Christ Jesus.

The apostle's prayer in Philippians 1:9-11 reminds us of the prayer in Colossians 1. He would have their love abound more and more in knowledge and all perception, or discernment. Brotherly love is not a matter of mere sentimentality; it is love in the truth. This calls for study of the Word of God in order that one may know just how to manifest that love on each particular occasion. Let us remember there is never a time when we are not called on to show love to our brother, but we cannot always manifest it in the same way if we are subject to the Word of God. We need instruction in the Word and enlightenment by the Holy Spirit so that we may perceive what is in accordance with the mind of God.

The first clause in Philippians 1:10—"That ye may approve things that are excellent"—is sometimes translated, "That ye may try the things that differ." The meaning is practically the same, for by testing things that differ, we approve what is excellent. The test is the Word of God. That Word is given to test all things and to manifest what is truly excellent. The Word explains to the believer how he should walk so that he can please God and be sincere and blameless in the day of Christ.

The Anglicized Latin word "sincere," which literally means "without wax," was used to translate a Greek word meaning "sun-tested" (Philippians 1:10). It might seem at first as though there is no connection between the Greek and Latin terms, but there is. The ancients had a very fine porcelain, which was greatly valued and brought a high price. This porcelain was so fragile that it was only with the greatest difficulty that it could be fired without being cracked. Dishonest dealers were in the habit of filling in the cracks with a pearly-white wax, which looked enough like true porcelain to pass without being readily detected in the shops. If the ware was held to the light, however, the wax at once became apparent as a dark seam. Honest Latin dealers marked their perfect wares *sine cera*, "without wax."

In the same manner the apostle would have the saints tested by the sunlight of God's truth and holiness, and found to be without wax; that is, he would have them be straightforward and honorable in all their dealings. Anything that savors of sham or hypocrisy is like the wax used to hide imperfections in the porcelain.

"Without offence" (or "blameless" as in Philippians 2:15) refers to motive, I take it. "Without offence" is not the same as "sinless," which would imply complete moral perfection. Blamelessness implies right motives.

"The fruits of righteousness" of Philippians 1:11 is the same as "the peaceable fruit of righteousness" of Hebrews 12:11, where the "fruit" is the result of being exercised under the hand of God. All righteousness is through Jesus Christ, for the glory and praise of God.

Joy in Evangelism (Philippians 1:12-20)

It is always a sad sign, an evidence of spiritual decline, when the heart loses its interest in the message of grace. Some are so occupied with the deeper truths of the Word of God that they allow themselves to speak slightingly of the simplicity of the gospel. Paul was the pre-eminent teacher of the church, but to his last hour his heart was filled with gospel zeal. His sympathies were with the evangelist carrying the word of life to men dead in trespasses and sins. Even in his prison house Paul rejoiced that his life had been devoted to the progress of the gospel.

Satan doubtless hoped to hinder Paul's evangelistic efforts by locking up the apostle in a jail, but even there it became obvious to caesar's court and all others that Paul's bonds were for Christ's sake. The very soldiers appointed to guard him heard the glorious proclamation of grace for a guilty world, and it is evident from Philippians 1:13 and 4:22 that numbers of them believed. Who can fathom the joy that must have filled the heart of Paul as he led one guard after another to the Savior's feet? Just as Paul and Silas were used in the conversion of their Philippian jailer and his household, so here grace triumphed over unfavorable circumstances. The prison cell in Rome became a gospel chapel where souls were born of God, and stern soldiers became captive servants of One greater than caesar.

In Philippians 1:14 the apostle spoke of another cause of joy. While he was going about from place to place preaching the word, there were gifted men who held back, thinking perhaps that they were in no sense on a par with him. They permitted the timidity and backwardness of the flesh to hinder their launching out in a work to which the Lord was beckoning them. But now that Paul was in prison and could no longer go about from place to place in this happy service, numbers of these men came forward and went forth preaching the word boldly and without fear.

On the other hand, there were some restless men who had not commended themselves as being fit for evangelistic work. While Paul was free, these men were kept in a place of subjection, but now that he was incarcerated they saw their opportunity to come to the front. They went forth preaching Christ with their lips, although their hearts were filled with envy and strife. But no jealous or envious thoughts entered the mind of Paul. He rejoiced in those who preached the word through goodwill and out of love, knowing that he was appointed for the vindication of the gospel, and although he could not rejoice in the spirit that moved the others, he was gladdened to know that it was Christ who was being preached. He was thankful for every voice telling out the story of the cross, and he would not permit anything to rob him of this joy.

The contrast is marked between the attitude of Paul and that which often prevails today. How seldom we see simple, unalloyed rejoicing that Christ is preached, whatever the aims and methods of the preacher are. Untold harm is often done by harsh, captious criticism of young and earnest men who perhaps have much to learn.

They may offend by their uncouthness and their lack of discernment and understanding of the ways of the Lord; nevertheless they preach Christ and win souls. God said, "He that winneth souls is wise," or as the Revised Version so strikingly puts it, "He that is wise winneth souls" (Proverbs 11:30).

Anxious young men have often been hindered by the criticism of their elders. Oh, for more of the spirit of Paul that would lead us to rejoice whenever Christ is preached! There may be much that exercises our hearts and leads us to prayer—and to godly admonition at times. But faulty methods and expressions, if rightly dealt with, may soon disappear as the earnest young evangelists grow in grace and in the knowledge of the truth.

In Philippians 1:19-20 we see how the apostle relied on the prayers of the people of God and how encouraged he was by the increase of gospel testimony. He felt that it foreshadowed his own deliverance and pointed to the time when he would again be free to preach Christ openly and widely according to his earnest expectation and hope. If that should not be the will of God, he would be free to glorify Him in a martyr's death. Paul had but one ambition: that Christ Himself should be magnified in his body, whether by life or by death. No matter what he might be called on to do or to suffer, if the One whom he had met on that unforgettable day on the Damascus turnpike were exalted and honored, he would be satisfied.

It is this utter absence of self-seeking that commends any true servant of Christ. We see such an attitude in John the Baptist, who said, "He must increase, but I must decrease" (John 3:30). It should be the supreme characteristic of the evangelist, pastor, or teacher. Where this spirit of self-abnegation for the glory of the Lord is really found, it commends the ministry, though it makes nothing of the minister. Oh, that we all might be more selfless!

Christ in Life or Death (Philippians 1:21-26)

The statement "To me to live is Christ" describes Christian life in all its fullness. It has often been remarked and is well worth remembering that Christians have many experiences in life that are not properly Christian experiences. The man described in Romans 7 is a

Christian who is in the midst of a conflict that will result in his future blessing, but the conflict itself is not properly Christian. In Philippians 1:21 Paul wrote of the life in which Christ so dominates and controls the believer that his one object is to live to His glory. This should be the experience of Christians at all times.

Unfortunately, few of us enter unreservedly into this life. It implies a surrendered will and a body yielded to the Lord who has redeemed it, that it may be used only to His praise. This is life in its truest sense, and probably no one ever entered into it so fully as the apostle Paul.

We may better understand the meaning of Philippians 1:21 if we consider for a moment what life means to many others. The christless businessman, whose one aim is to obtain wealth, might well say, "To me to live is money." The careless seeker after the world's pleasures, if he told the truth, would say, "To me to live is worldly pleasure." The carnal individual, given to luxurious living and self-gratification, would say, "To me to live is self." The politician, exulting in the plaudits of the people and craving notoriety, might declare, "To me to live is fame and power." But Paul could say, and every Christian should be able to say, "To me to live is Christ."

Only those who are able to say, "To me to live is Christ," can heartily add, "and to die is gain." Death is no enemy to the one to whom Christ is all. If he lives, he has opportunity to manifest Christ down here; if he dies, he is with Christ, and nothing could be more precious than that.

The apostle himself was in a dilemma as to whether he would prefer life or death, were the choice left to him. If permitted to continue in the body, he would have further opportunity for service for Him who had claimed him as His own and called him to the ministry. On the other hand, he longed "to depart, and to be with Christ; which is far better" (Philippians 1:23). Paul's life had been one of toil and suffering for Christ's sake, such as only a Spirit-sustained man could have endured without fainting.

As the apostle lay in a Roman prison, his heart longed for release, a release that would mean to be forever with Christ. Labor for Christ was sweet, but rest with Christ would be sweeter. Whitefield used to say, "I am often weary *in* the work, but never weary *of* it."

Such was the attitude of Paul. He loved to serve, yet he longed too for the hour of release. His motive was not selfish, for his one object was Christ, whether in life or in death.

It is amazing how anyone who has read Philippians 1:23 could question for a moment that the Word of God teaches the consciousness of the spirit after death. Paul had no thought that his spirit would be buried with his body in the grave, or that his soul would sleep until the resurrection day. Death to him would be a departure, an exodus, a moving out of the travel-worn earthly tabernacle and a going to be with Christ until the first resurrection at the coming of the Lord.

As he weighed the pros and cons, he revealed his unselfishness. He saw the need of the church of God. As it is now, so it was then. There were many evangelists, but few teachers and pastors who really carried the people of God on their hearts. For this reason Paul felt that to remain alive for the sake of the flock was more important than to seek eternal rest for himself. So he said he had confidence that he would remain here a little longer for the "furtherance and joy of faith" of God's people (Philippians 1:25).

I think Paul fully expected the Lord to permit him to revisit Philippi so that the saints there would rejoice more abundantly in Christ Jesus. They were his children in the faith and as a tender father he longed to see them once more before closing his earthly ministry. We have no record in the Word of God as to whether this desire was fulfilled, but there are early church traditions which indicate that it was. We know he was released from his first imprisonment and allowed to go about in freedom for several years before being apprehended again and martyred for the sake of our Lord Jesus. Paul followed Him even to death.

Unity in Evangelism (Philippians 1:27-30)

The word "conversation" (Philippians 1:27) had a broader meaning in Paul's day than it does today. It referred to behavior in general, not just the talk of the lips. The apostle's exhortation meant that the entire manner of life of the people of God should be in accordance with the gospel of Christ.

No more important message was ever committed to man than the word of reconciliation, which God has graciously entrusted to His people in this present dispensation of His mercy to a lost world. That gospel tells of the divine means of deliverance from the guilt and power of sin. How incongruous, then, are the testimonies of those who undertake to proclaim that message with their mouths, but deny its power in their lives! A walk worthy of the gospel is a walk in the energy of the Holy Spirit; it is a life surrendered to Him, whose lordship the gospel declares.

In Philippians 1:27-30 the apostle was not referring merely to our individual responsibility to walk worthy of the gospel. As he wrote this passage he was concerned with assembly responsibility. He wished to hear that the Philippians as an assembly were standing fast in one spirit and with one mind, cooperating vigorously for the faith of the gospel.

Nothing so mars gospel testimony as contention and self-seeking among God's people. Contentious Christians discredit the message they profess to love. When jealousies and envyings come in to hinder the fellowship of those who should be standing together heart to heart and shoulder to shoulder for the truth of God, the effect on the world outside is most lamentable. Unsaved members of believers' families are particularly affected. Nothing is more harmful to them than to find out that their elders are not unitedly standing together for the Word of God.

Is there not something in this passage that deserves the careful consideration of present-day believers who gather in the name of the Lord Jesus Christ? Have we not allowed personalities, bickerings, and strife to mar and hinder gospel testimony?

Contention in the local church may impede the work of the evangelist. On the other hand, it must be confessed that some who possess the gift of evangelism have ignored to a marked degree the importance of fellowship in gospel testimony. They have launched forth without the prayerful endorsement of older, more godly saints and afterward have been surprised and grieved over not finding heartier cooperation in the churches whose judgment they ignored in the beginning.

The evangelist is the Lord's servant and therefore not subject to human dictation. But fellowship involves mutual responsibility, and evangelists need to remember that the gift of evangelism is not necessarily accompanied by piety and does not always carry with it good judgment and sound wisdom. It is important for the evangelist to cultivate humility if he wants to have the hearty fellowship of assemblies of believers.

When a humble spirit is manifested by the evangelist and there is vigorous cooperation on the part of a local church, God can be depended on to work in mighty power for the salvation of lost souls and the blessing of His people. This is a combination the enemy dreads. When those in an assembly of believers are walking in love and are exercised about the Lord's things, they need not fear the attacks of evil powers—natural or supernatural—from without. The unholy hosts read their own doom in the happy fellowship of the saints of God and see in it a proof of the truth of the Lord's words: "Upon this rock I will build my church; and the gates of hell shall not prevail against it" (Matthew 16:18).

The thought that many seem to have in mind when reading Matthew 16:18 is that the church of God is like a city besieged, beleaguered by the enemies of the Lord and carrying on a defensive warfare, albeit with the pledge of eventual victory. But this is not the picture presented by our Lord. An invading or besieging army does not carry the gates of its cities with it. It is Hell, or Hades, or the realm of darkness that is being besieged by the forces of light who are carrying on not a defensive warfare, but an offensive warfare. To them the promise is given that "the gates of hell shall not prevail." This is the "perdition" spoken of in Philippians 1:28.

Fellowship in this offensive warfare cannot be fully experienced apart from suffering, but this is to be esteemed a privilege by those who fight under the banner of the risen Lord. It is given to such warriors, as a reward greatly to be desired, not only to trust in Christ as Savior, but also to toil manfully and to suffer that His name may be glorified in the place where He was rejected and crucified, and over which He soon will be coming to reign.

How blessedly and how fully the apostle entered into this toil and suffering! With joy he endured and suffered so that Christ might be glorified. Even at the time he wrote this letter he was a prisoner for the Lord in a Roman jail. Meanwhile some of the saints at Philippi were living in lazy comfort and stooping to quarrel among themselves. Paul's words in Philippians 1:30 would surely stir their hearts and consciences as they contrasted their easy lives with the sufferings of Christ's dear servant, who was in prison because of his unselfish devotion to the Lord he loved. May we learn to walk in the same spirit and mind the same things.

CHAPTER TWO
CHRIST, THE BELIEVER'S EXAMPLE

The Lowly Mind (Philippians 2:1-4)

The last word of Philippians 2:4 is the keynote of this section: "others." The overpowering, dominating note in the life of our Lord on earth was "others," and because of "others" He died. He "came not to be ministered unto, but to minister, and to give his life a ransom for [others]" (Mark 10:45). He lived for others; He died for others. He did not know what selfishness was. Unselfish devotion for the good of others summed up His entire life, which was lived wholly in subjection to the Father's will.

God the Father Himself lives, reverently be it said, for others. He finds His delight, His joy, in lavishing blessings on others. He pours His rain and sends His sunshine on the just and the unjust alike. He gave His Son for others. And having not withheld His own Son, but having "delivered him up for us all, how shall he not with him also freely give us all things?" (Romans 8:32).

We are included in the "others" for whom the Lord Jesus Christ endured so much. It is not surprising then that if we follow His steps, we will find ourselves called on to live for others and even to lay down our lives for them.

In Philippians 2:1 the word "if" does not imply that there might not be consolation in Christ, comfort of love, fellowship of the Spirit, and tender mercies. Rather, "if" has the intensive force of the word *since.* Paul was saying, "Since you know there are consolations and

31

comforts in Christ..." How incongruous it is for believers to act as though these blessed realities are nonexistent! Drinking in the spirit of Christ, we exemplify the mind of Christ. And so the apostle exhorted the saints in Philippi to fill his cup of joy by being likeminded, of one accord, with equal love toward one another.

Christians will never see eye to eye on all points. We are so largely influenced by habits, environment, education, and our level of intellectual and spiritual understanding that we could never look at everything from the same standpoint. How then can we be of one mind? The apostle himself explained it elsewhere when he said, "We have the mind of Christ" (1 Corinthians 2:16). The "mind of Christ" is the lowly mind. If we are all of this mind, we will walk together in love, considering one another and seeking to help each other's faith rather than to challenge each other's convictions.

The lowly mind is emphasized in Philippians 2:3: "Let nothing be done through strife or vainglory." It is possible, as Philippians 1:15-16 has already shown us, to be controlled by a competitive, boastful spirit even in connection with the holy things of the Lord. But Paul's own attitude is a beautiful example of the lowliness of mind of which he spoke: he could rejoice even though Christ was preached "of contention."

Nothing is less suited to a follower of the meek and lowly Son of man than a contentious spirit and vainglorious bearing. Boasting and bitter words ill-become one who has taken the place of death with Christ. If, in lowliness of mind, each esteems others better than himself, it is impossible for strife and contention to come in. Unfortunately it is much easier to speak or write of the lowly mind than to demonstrate it.

Natural man is not capable of following Paul's advice here. The man after the flesh looks out for Number One and is fond of reminding himself and others that charity begins at home. But the Christian is exhorted to look not on his own things, but on the things of others. This is a heavenly principle and can only be followed by a heavenly person, one who walks in fellowship with Him who came from Heaven to show His love for others. It is characteristic of man's deceitful natural heart to suppose that he will find his greatest pleasure in ministering to his own desires. But the truest happiness is the result of unselfish devotion to the things of others. If this fact were always kept in mind, many of God's dear children would be spared numerous unhappy experiences, and their fellowship in Christ would become glad and joyous.

The Relinquishment of Prerogatives (Philippians 2:5-8)

We now consider one of the most sublime and wonderful mysteries in all Scripture. Theologians have called this mystery the doctrine of the "kenosis." The title comes from the Greek expression that is translated "made himself of no reputation" in Philippians 2:7. The expression really means "emptied himself" or "divested himself."

Note that doctrines are never presented in Scripture merely as dogmas to be accepted by the faithful if they want to avoid expulsion from the Christian company. The most important doctrines are introduced by the Holy Spirit in an exceedingly natural way. I do not use the word *natural* here in contrast to the word *spiritual,* but rather in the sense of "sequence to the subject" or "without special emphasis." The doctrine of our Lord's self-emptying is presented simply as the supreme illustration of the lowliness of mind that should characterize all who profess to be followers of the Savior. The doctrine follows naturally after the exhortation of Philippians 2:4.

Paul introduced the subject in Philippians 2:5: "Let this mind be in you, which was also in Christ Jesus." "This mind" is the lowly mind, for it is written, "Even Christ pleased not himself" (Romans 15:3).

Immediately after introducing the subject, Paul provided the example of Christ. He existed throughout eternity in the form of God. Philippians 2:6 is a declaration of His true deity, for no mere creature could exist in the form of God. Lucifer aspired to this and for his impiety was hurled down from the archangel's throne. Our Lord Jesus Christ has claim to deity because He is the eternal Son. He thought of equality with God not as a thing to be grasped or held onto.

Equal with God He is, but Christ chose to take the place of subjection and lowliness. He chose to step down from the sublime height that belonged to Him, even the glory which He had with the Father before the world was (see John 17:5), and take the servant's form to do the Father's will.

The first man aspired to be as God and fell. The Second Man, the Lord from Heaven, came down from His eternal throne. As we sing, "From Godhead's fullest glory / He came to bear our woe" (A. Stevenson). Christ did not retain the outward semblance of deity. He relinquished His rightful position to become the Savior of sinners. In order to do this He emptied Himself, or divested Himself, of His divine prerogatives.

Let there be no misunderstanding. While we reverently take off our shoes and draw near to behold this great sight, let us not fear to accept the declaration of Holy Scripture in all its fullness. He divested Himself of something—but of what? Not of His deity, for that could not be. He was always a divine person, the Son of the Father. He could unite manhood and deity, but He could not cease to be divine. Of what, then, did He divest Himself? He divested Himself of His rights as God the Son. He chose to come to earth to take a place of subjection. He took on Himself "the form of a servant, and was made in the likeness of men" (Philippians 2:7).

Observe the distinction brought out in verses 6 and 7: He existed from all eternity in the form of God; He came here to take the form of a servant. Angels are servants, but "he took not on him the nature of angels" (Hebrews 2:16). He came in the likeness of men. His coming was all voluntary and as a man on earth He chose to be guided by the Holy Spirit. He received daily from the Father, through the Word of God, the instruction that a man should receive. His mighty works of power were not wrought by His own divine omnipotence alone. He chose that they should be wrought in the power of the Holy Spirit. This is the precious and important doctrine of the kenosis as revealed in Scripture.

Men have added to this what Scripture does not say. They have declared that when He came to earth, Christ ceased to be God, that He became an ignorant Galilean peasant. Suppose this were the case. His knowledge of divine mysteries would have been no greater than what might have been expected of any other good man of His generation. His testimony as to the inspiration of Scripture would have had no real weight. He would not have known more than others of His day knew. He would have not been competent to speak about the authors of the Old Testament books.

Today's wiseacres do not hesitate to declare that Jesus was wrong to think that Daniel wrote the book that bears his name and that Moses penned the Pentateuch. Their false declaration is based on a false interpretation of the kenosis. They say that Christ emptied Himself of His divine knowledge and therefore could not have spoken with authority.

The Exaltation of Christ (Philippians 2:9-11)

The exaltation of the man Christ Jesus is the glorious fulfillment of the prophecy of Psalm 110, a prophecy used by our Lord to confound His critics. They professed to be waiting for the promised Messiah, but rejected His deity. The Psalm begins, "The Lord said unto my Lord, Sit thou at my right hand, until I make thine enemies thy footstool." Christ is David's Son, yet David called Him Lord because He is the Root of David. Jesus descended from Jesse's son, yet the son of Jesse came into being through Him.

Christ's exaltation as man to the throne of God is not only Jehovah's attestation of perfect satisfaction in His work, but also the recognition of His equality with Himself. This man, who had humbled Himself to the extent of going to the death of the cross, is Jehovah's "fellow," as Zechariah 13:7 declares. Such language could be rightly used only in reference to a divine person.

It is interesting to notice that God never permitted one indignity to be put on the body of His Son after His work was finished—after the Roman soldier, having pierced His side, released the atoning blood. Thereafter no enemies' hands touched His body. Loving disciples tenderly took it down from the cross, wrapped it in linen clothes, and reverently laid it in Joseph's new tomb.

Then, when the appointed time had passed, He who had died came forth in resurrection life and God the Father received Him up into glory. He has "highly exalted him, and given him a name which is above every name" (Philippians 2:9). Christ is the pre-eminent One in every sphere.

How appropriate that His glory should answer to His shame. "As many were astonished at Him...so shall He astonish many nations" (literal rendering of Isaiah 52:14-15). God has ordained it, and so it must be. At the name of *Jesus*—His personal name which means "Jehovah-the-Savior," the name on the placard nailed above His head as He hung on the cross—every knee will bow. Every heavenly, earthly, and infernal being must own Him Lord of all.

Observe that in this passage where the authority of Christ is being recognized, the three spheres of Heaven, earth, and Hell are mentioned, indicating that all created intelligent beings will bow to Him. There will be no exceptions. All must confess His lordship to the glory of God the Father. All must bow in lowly submissiveness at the mention of the name of the crucified One.

Does this passage imply universal salvation and the final restoration of Satan and his hosts, as some have taught? Surely not. Subjugation is one thing; reconciliation is another. When the latter is in question, we have only two spheres mentioned, as in Colossians 1:20: "Having made peace through the blood of his cross, by him to reconcile all things unto himself; by him, I say, whether they be things in earth, or things in heaven." Here there is no mention of the underworld. The lost will never be reconciled. Heaven and earth eventually will be filled with happy beings who have been redeemed to God by the precious blood of Christ. Then reconciliation will be complete.

But "under the earth" will be those who have their part in the outer darkness, the lake of fire (see Revelation 21:8). They flaunted Christ's authority on earth, so they will have to acknowledge it in Hell. They refused to heed the call of grace and be reconciled to God in the day when they might have been saved. In the pit of woe no gospel message will ever be proclaimed, but the authority of the Lord Jesus Christ will be supremely enforced. There will be no disorder in Hell; no further rebellion will be permitted. All must bow at the name of Jesus and every tongue must confess Him Lord. Scripture depicts no wild pandemonium when it describes the abode of the lost.

How blessed it is to acknowledge His lordship now! As it is written, "If thou shalt confess with thy mouth the Lord Jesus, and shalt believe in thine heart that God hath raised him from the dead, thou shalt be saved. For with the heart man believeth unto righteousness; and with the mouth confession is made unto salvation" (Romans 10:9-10). How fitting it is that only those who confess Him now will be eternally saved as a result of the work of the cross.

The Testimony of the Assembly (Philippians 2:12-16)

Having dealt with the self-abnegation of our Lord Jesus Christ, Paul went on, as guided by the Holy Spirit, to apply this truth in a practical way in the balance of the chapter. Verses 12-16 refer to assembly life and responsibility. Verses 17-30 bring three men before us; these were seeking to display in their lives the devotedness and self-denying concern for others that were seen in Christ as man on earth.

Philippians 2:12 has often perplexed those who thought they saw clearly from Scripture the simplicity of salvation by grace, apart from works. Here, in seeming contrast to that doctrine, the apostle told the saints to work out their own salvation with fear and trembling, as though there were a possibility that salvation might be forfeited because of failure to work it out properly.

Notice first, however, that the apostle did not speak of working *for* salvation. He spoke of working it *out,* which is very different. I am reminded of a little girl who listened to a legalistic sermon preached on this text. The minister insisted that no one could be saved by grace alone; each person must work out his own salvation. At the close of the service she innocently asked, "Mother, how can you work it out if you haven't got it in?"

If salvation of the individual were being contemplated here, it might be enough of an explanation to say, "It is your own; therefore manifest it—work it out." But more than individual salvation is being contemplated. Taken in context, verse 12 refers to assembly salvation. That is, Paul was giving direction to an assembly of Christians. They were exposed to difficulties from without and from within; they were passing through a world totally opposed to the testimony committed to them. Paul was showing them how to continue in fellowship together in spite of the fact that each individual had within him a corrupt nature that could surface—to the detriment of the whole church—if given the opportunity.

We have already noticed that there was some difficulty in the Philippian assembly between two sisters of prominence, Euodias and Syntyche. This disagreement could easily cause distressing quarrels and even division if not judged in the presence of the Lord. Similar misunderstandings could arise from time to time and would need to be carefully watched for. When the apostle himself was with the Philippians, they could refer all such matters to him and he would, so to speak, work out their salvation from these perplexities. He would advise and guide as needed. But at the time he was writing to them, he was far away. He was a prisoner for the gospel's sake and could not personally give the help he wanted to provide. Since he was absent, he directed them as obedient children to work out their own salvation in godly fear and with exercise of soul, so that they would not depart from the right path or stray out of the will of God.

How beneficial Paul's words have been for generations of Christians! Sooner or later, all assemblies of saints on earth will probably have internal differences, and the advice or command the apostle gave to the Philippians will apply in all such cases. It is God's way that churches should be put right from within, by self-judgment in His presence and submission to His Word.

How often saints take the very opposite approach! Questions arise to trouble and perplex; differences of judgment occur; bickerings and quarrels begin. Instead of coming together in the presence of God for humiliation and guidance, and seeking His mind from His own Word and acting accordingly, they appeal to an outsider for help. Often as a result matters only get more complicated. Perhaps the church appeals to someone engaged in a traveling ministry and requests him to adjudicate. Such an approach often disturbs the spirit of the visitor and cannot really save the local fellowship from the troubles that have arisen.

It is easy to see how the clerical system arose from such experiences. We see in the early church men such as Diotrephes, who loved to have the pre-eminence (see 3 John 9), and the Nicolaitanes (rulers of the people), who sought to bring the saints into bondage.

When such men caused problems, believers generally found it much easier to apply to noted preachers or teachers for help than to cast themselves directly on God and His Word. Thus gifted men became a sort of court of appeals and eventually were recognized as the clergy.

Dependence on others easily creeps in wherever saints look to men rather than to God and His Word. If you think a group of Christians are too ignorant to know how to settle their own differences, remember that they have God and the Word of His Grace. If they humble themselves, wait on Him, and refuse to move until they find direction in the Book, God can be depended on to help them work out their own salvation from whatever perplexing circumstances have arisen. He casts them not on their own resources, but on His Word and on Himself, who works in them the will to do His good pleasure. This does not mean that they should ignore or despise the advice and sound judgment of others, but they should not be dependent on it.

In Philippians 2:14-16 we see the working out of assembly salvation practically demonstrated. Murmurings and disputings must be judged in the presence of God. Instead of backbiting and gossiping, saints should come together before the Lord and deal with problems in the light of His revealed Word. Then they will indeed be "blameless and harmless, the sons of God, without rebuke." They will walk in a manner worthy of the Lord in the midst of a crooked and perverse generation among whom they will shine as lights in this dark world. Having judged whatever was hindering fellowship within, the saints will be in a condition to be a testimony to the power of grace to those outside.

As the apostle emphasized in Philippians 1, nothing so delivers believers from self-occupation as occupation with Christ and the presentation of Christ to those still in their sins. Those who are busy presenting the word of life to others have no time for selfish quarreling among themselves.

Paul told the saints at Philippi that if they walked worthily, they would bring joy to his heart and he would be able to rejoice in the day of Christ. That is, at the judgment seat it would be evident that his labors in Philippi had not been in vain. Godly order and devoted gospel testimony would witness to the reality of the work of God in and among them.

Thus we see that working out our own salvation is simply submitting to the truth of God after we have been saved. Whether as individuals or as assemblies of saints in the place of testimony, we submit to the truth in order to glorify Him. We will work out our salvation "with fear and trembling" as we realize our liability to err, the faultiness of our understanding, and the holiness of the One whom we are called to serve.

The Example of Paul (Philippians 2:17-18)

The apostolic writer went on to cite, though in an apparently casual way, three examples of men who exemplified the spirit of Christ—men of like passions with their fellow believers. First he referred to himself. Later he referred to the lowly ways and devoted service of Timothy and Epaphroditus.

Possibly no other mortal man ever drank into the spirit of Christ so deeply as the great apostle to the Gentiles. Once he was a proud, haughty Pharisee, glorying in his own righteousness, burning with indignant bigotry against any who claimed to have received a higher revelation than what was found in Judaism. Then as he was hurrying to Damascus to apprehend any who confessed the name of Jesus, this religious persecutor was transformed by a vision of the glorified Christ. The sight of the once-crucified but now-enthroned Savior at God's right hand, was the means of a conversion so radical and so sudden that probably no other experience since has been so intense.

From that moment, the one desire overpowering all else, the inmost yearning of his being, was to reveal Christ in all his ways. Paul was not an absolutely sinless man; neither was he without the infirmities common to the human race. But he was one who always sought to judge himself in the light of the cross of Christ and with the power of Christ resting on him. The apostle's entire philosophy of life is summed up in his fervent words to the Galatians: "God forbid that I should glory, save in the cross of our Lord Jesus Christ, by whom the world is crucified unto me, and I unto the world" (Galatians 6:14).

In this spirit Paul wrote to his beloved Philippians, "Yea, and if I be offered [poured out] upon the sacrifice and service of your faith, I joy, and rejoice with you all" (Philippians 2:17). He had just told them that his joy in the day of Christ would be to find them approved, having walked before God as unrebuked saints earnestly engaged in holding forth the word of life in a dark world. Paul would look on their abundant service and their reward as a reward to himself. He would feel that he had not run in vain or labored in vain. He was willing to count all his service as an adjunct of theirs—to have their labors and devotedness looked on as the completion of a work that he had merely begun.

In order to understand verse 17 properly, it is necessary to observe carefully what the apostle had in mind. When he said, "If I be poured out upon the sacrifice of your faith," he was alluding to the drink offering. This was a cup of wine that was poured out on a burnt offering and was a type of the outpouring of our Lord Jesus Christ's soul unto death. The drink offering symbolized the voluntary surrender of everything that might naturally be expected to contribute to his joys as a man, for wine is the symbol of gladness. What man ever deserved to be happier than the Lord Jesus Christ? To whom was gladness a righteous due, if not to Him? Yet in infinite grace He became "a man of sorrows, and acquainted with grief" (Isaiah 53:3).

The burnt offering pictured Christ offering Himself without spot to God on our behalf. In the sacrificial service, the animal slain for a burnt offering was cut into pieces, washed with water, then laid in order on the fire of the altar and wholly consumed. The drink offering was poured on the burnt offering and in a moment was lost to sight.

With all this in mind, consider the beauty of the figure the apostle employed. Whatever service the Philippians might be able to render to the Lord would be rendered in fellowship with Christ. Thus their devotion could be viewed as an offering or a sacrifice to God. The sweet-smelling savor of their sacrifice was the result of lives surrendered to the Lord. Paul was willing to have his labor looked on as simply the drink offering poured on their burnt offering.

What sublime self-abnegation! What delight in the labors of others! We notice the absence of that which is so abhorrent in professedly Christian service today. Laborers sometimes are jealous of the ministry of others and envious of success in which they think they have not shared. There was no such spirit in the apostle Paul. He rejoiced in everything that the Lord did through others and his jealousy was only for the glory of God. In this he followed Christ, and so he could confidently appeal to the Philippians to follow him as he walked in His steps. He wanted them to rejoice with him in their mutual devotedness.

It is significant that Paul spoke of himself and his service in an incidental way and in just one verse. When he wrote about his fellow laborer Timothy and their messenger Epaphroditus, he had much more to say. He could dwell with delight on the labors and service of others, but when writing of himself, he felt as if he were speaking like a fool (see 2 Corinthians 11:23).

The Example of Timothy (Philippians 2:19-24)

Paul was not only a fervent evangelist; he was also the prince of teachers and, like his fellow-apostle Peter, a true pastor or shepherd of the flock of Christ. In this latter respect the young preacher Timothy was Paul's ardent imitator.

Whatever other gifts Timothy may have had, one special gift was probably given to him at the laying on of hands when the elders sent him out to do the work of the Lord: the gift of pastor. This is perhaps one of the rarest and yet one of the most needed of all the gifts given by an ascended Christ for the edification of His church. The evangelist ministers to those without Christ. The teacher instructs those already saved. The pastor is more concerned about the state of the soul of the believer than the state of his knowledge of abstract truth. Of course pastors should recognize that saints are formed by the truth and that a right state of soul and a walk in the truth go together.

Paul was anxious to send Timothy to Philippi so that he could be a help and a means of blessing to the flock there. The apostle trusted that Timothy might be used by God to weld the hearts of the Philippian believers into one and to deliver them from the dissension that had resulted from the misunderstanding between Euodias and Syntyche. Paul felt that he could depend on Timothy's judgment, and he counted on being comforted himself when he actually knew the state of the souls of his friends.

Our standing before God is one thing; our actual state is another. Paul was concerned about the latter. Other than Timothy, the apostle did not know of anyone with an unselfish shepherd-heart who would wholeheartedly care for the state of the Philippians. The word "naturally" in verse 20 does not adequately convey Paul's thought. Timothy's pastoral concern was not a gift of nature, but a spiritual gift. As a result of the exercise of his soul before God, his entire being was stirred with concern for the Lord's people. Others may have been gifted in various ways, but of them the apostle could only sadly say, "All seek their own, not the things which are Jesus Christ's" (Philippians 2:21).

It is quite possible to be an admired teacher on whose words thousands hang and yet be a vain self-seeker. It is possible to be an eloquent evangelist and yet be using the very gift that God has given for personal aggrandizement. Eager multitudes may flock to listen with delight to the messages of a man who professes to care little or nothing for money but is using his gift of evangelism to obtain wealth. However, the more marked the pastoral gift, the more unselfishly devoted the servant must be. The pastor's great ambition will be to feed the flock and shield them from danger.

The patriarch Jacob is an apt illustration of the true shepherd. In spite of all his failures and the fact that he was under the discipline of God through the greater part of his life, Jacob was a lover of the flock and always considerate of their interests. As he looked back over his years of caring for the sheep, he could honestly say to his father-in-law Laban, "Thus I was; in the day the drought consumed me, and the frost by night; and my sleep departed from mine eyes" (Genesis 31:40). When Esau wanted Jacob and his host to hurry on, Jacob expostulated with his brother: "My lord knoweth that the children are tender, and the flocks and herds with young are with me: and if men should overdrive them one day, all the flock will die" (Genesis 33:13). A Diotrephes might try to cajole or coerce the flock into submission to his own imperious will, but a God-appointed shepherd will seek to lead on safely, wearing himself out for the blessing of others. He will seek not to impose his own will, but to serve the Lord and exalt Him.

As a son with a father, Timothy had commended himself to the aged apostle by serving with him in the gospel in lowliness and humility. Youth is often exceedingly energetic and impatient of restraint, while age is inclined perhaps to be overcautious and slow in coming to conclusions. So it is often difficult for two people, so wide apart in years as Paul and Timothy were, to labor together happily. But when the younger man exhibits a humble spirit and the elder seeks only the glory of God and the blessing of His people, fellowship in service is possible and indeed is blessed.

Since Timothy had proven himself, Paul could trust him with a mission such as the apostle had in mind. Paul was waiting to learn the outcome of his appeal to caesar, and then he hoped to send Timothy to Philippi to be a healer of dissensions and thus a means of cheer and consolation to the fellowship.

Timothy followed Paul as Paul followed Christ. Thus Timothy became the second of the three servants who were worthy to be held up as examples of those who manifested the mind of Christ.

It was the apostle's desire and hope to visit his beloved Philippians again later on. Whether this yearning was ever fulfilled we will not know until all is revealed at the judgment seat of Christ. Precious is the faith that can leave everything with Him, assured that His ways are always perfect and always best.

The Example of Epaphroditus (Philippians 2:25-30)

It was Epaphroditus who had brought the bounty of the Philippian saints to Paul, their father in Christ. Burning with love toward the Lord's dear servant who was shut up in prison for the gospel's sake, he took the long journey from Macedonia to Rome. We have no way now of knowing whether Epaphroditus journeyed by land or sea, but we know he traveled to the world's metropolis in order to assure the prisoner of the love and esteem of the church at Philippi and to supply his needs with their gift.

Having accomplished his purpose, Epaphroditus became ill, possibly overcome by the Roman fever that was so dangerous for unacclimated strangers. That his illness was a protracted one is evident because before he recovered, word of his condition reached the Philippians and a return message got back to him. The message expressed their solicitude for his health and their anxiety that he be restored to them again. Notice that Epaphroditus did not seem to be as concerned about his illness as he was about their distress. He was one of those thoroughly self-denying men whose motto might well be "Others."

He recovered from his sickness, and although it must have been difficult for him to leave the apostle in prison, Epaphroditus was anxious to be on his way. He wanted to comfort the Philippians by his presence and bring them Paul's Epistle. Apparently acting as secretary, Epaphroditus wrote the apostle's words down and then carried the precious parchment to Philippi. Thus he preserved the letter for us and for all saints to the end of time—and, we may say, forever.

We know nothing about Epaphroditus except what is recorded in this letter. Some, however, think he is to be identified with the Epaphras mentioned in the Epistle to the Colossians. *Epaphroditus* means "favored of Aphrodite," the Greek goddess of love and beauty, also known in Rome as Venus. His name indicates that he had heathen parents, but he had come to know Christ. *Epaphras*—said to be a diminutive of *Epaphroditus* with the name of the heathen goddess omitted—means simply "graced" or "favored."

Having been won to Christ, Epaphroditus was characterized by a godly zeal to make Him known to others and to build up and lead on those already saved. This devoted messenger was the exemplification of the mind of Christ, as described in the beginning of this chapter. He may not have been physically strong, but he was a man who did not spare himself. In the work of Christ he became sick and almost died.

Sickness is not always the result of sin, as some have taught. In the case of this man of God, sickness was the result of his self-denying activity on behalf of those to whom he ministered. His illness was the cause of deep sorrow to Paul and no doubt led to much prayer on his behalf. God answered, showing mercy, and raised him up.

The apostle did not think that he had any right to demand physical healing even for so faithful a laborer as Epaphroditus. Paul recognized healing as evidence of the mercy of God, not as that to which saints have a right. This is true divine healing. And let it be remembered that sickness as well as health may be from God. It is clear that Paul never believed or taught "healing in the atonement" as the birthright privilege of all Christians. Nor do we ever read of him or his fellow laborers being healed miraculously. Paul, Trophimus, Timothy, and Epaphroditus all bear witness to the contrary.

The apostle urged the saints in Philippi to receive their messenger with gladness when he returned to them and commanded them to hold him in high esteem because he had been deathly ill for the cause of Christ. Epaphroditus had risked his own life in order to serve Paul in their stead.

Men such as Epaphroditus are those whom God delights to honor. Like the Lord Jesus, Epaphroditus made himself of no reputation, and because of his very lowliness he is to be held in high regard. Those who believe themselves to be worthy of honor and esteem are not the ones whom God calls the saints to recognize. Rather, those who are willing to take the lowly path and not seek great things for themselves are the ones whom the Lord will exalt in due time.

Beneficial lessons can be learned from the lives of the three devoted men of God on whose self-denying ways we have meditated. May we have grace to follow the examples of Paul, Timothy, and Epaphroditus as they followed the example of Christ.

CHAPTER THREE
CHRIST, THE BELIEVER'S OBJECT

The Epistle of Joy (Philippians 3:1-3)

Careful students of Paul's Epistles will notice the frequent occurrence of parenthetical passages. In Philippians, for example, it seems that the apostle was about to conclude abruptly in 3:1, for he had completed the main part of his treatise, but suddenly he was moved by the Spirit of God to launch into an altogether different topic. So he added a kind of parenthesis before he actually finished his letter.

Another example is seen in the Epistle to the Ephesians. All of chapter 3, after verse 1, is parenthetical, and in chapter 4 he concluded what he had started to say in 3:1. (Compare Ephesians 3:1 and 4:1.)

In Philippians 3:1 Paul wrote, "Finally, my brethren." Yet in 4:8 where he introduced his closing remarks, he used the same expression: "Finally, brethren." All of chapter 3 is a new subject, a message for which we can truly thank God, for we would have lost much precious ministry if it had been omitted.

It has often been said that this letter to the Philippians is the Epistle of joy, and indeed it is. As the apostle wrote, his heart was filled with the joyful recollection of his past experiences in scenes so dear to him. He wanted his fellow believers in Philippi to complete his joy by sharing with him in the gladness that was his in Christ, so he exhorted them to "rejoice in the Lord" (Philippians 3:1). Circumstances may be anything but conducive to either peace or gladness, yet the trusting soul can always look above the restlessness of earth

47

to the throne where Christ sits exalted as Lord at God's right hand. He is over all.

There are no second causes with Him. "Shall there be evil in a city, and the Lord hath not done it?" asked the prophet (Amos 3:6). This Old Testament verse refers to evil, not in the sense of sin, but in the sense of calamity, even if that calamity is the result of sin. Calamity cannot come unless it is permitted by the Lord. Knowing that "all things work together for good to them that love God, to them who are the called according to his purpose" (Romans 8:28), why should the believer either doubt or fear? Waves may roll high, stormy winds may beat tempestuously, and all to which the heart has clung may be swept away, but Christ abides unchanged and unchangeable, the everlasting portion of those who trust His grace.

When the people spoke of stoning David because of a calamitous event for which they held him largely responsible, he "encouraged himself in the Lord his God" (1 Samuel 30:6). "The joy of the Lord is your strength," Nehemiah reminded the remnant of Israel (Nehemiah 8:10). Before returning to the Father's house from which He came, the Lord Jesus imparted His joy to the trembling company of His disciples.

It is not only the Christian's privilege, but also his duty to rejoice constantly in the Lord. Holiness and happiness are intimately linked. How often we need to be reminded to rejoice, as the apostle reminded the Philippians. For our own well-being we should frequently be exhorted to "rejoice in the Lord."

In Philippians 3:2, the Holy Spirit guided Paul to introduce an entirely new subject. The significant word "beware" is found three times in this verse, for our busy enemy has so many agencies through which he seeks to rob us of the joy that is our rightful portion.

"Beware of dogs," said Paul. "Dogs" was the abusive and disrespectful title the Jew used when speaking of the Gentiles who did not bear in their bodies the mark of the Abrahamic covenant. In the Old Testament God used the term to distinguish false pastors or shepherds in Israel: "His watchmen are blind: they are all ignorant, they are all dumb dogs, they cannot bark; sleeping, lying down, loving to slumber. Yea, they are greedy dogs which can never have enough, and they are shepherds that cannot understand: they all look to their own way, every one for his gain, from his quarter" (Isaiah 56:10-11). In the New Testament Peter used the dog as a symbol of the false religious teacher who is going back to the things he once professed to abhor: "The dog is turned to his own vomit again" (2 Peter 2:22).

The Philippians, like the early Christians in general, were exposed to the ravages of such "dogs." Evil teachers from Judaism were among the flock of Christ for the purpose of perverting the saints and leading them back into bondage. These "dogs" were motivated by their own selfish ends and thus the Holy Spirit referred to them with an opprobrious term. They introduced themselves in the assemblies of believers in order to tear apart the flock of Christ and gain special recognition as leaders in the new company. Professing to be ministers of Christ, they were in reality servants of Satan, as their works proved. They had no heart for the afflicted sheep and lambs for whom Christ died. These "dogs" fed themselves and not the flock, and their judgment is assured.

Paul added, "Beware of evil workers." We do not need to distinguish "evil workers" from "dogs," for false teachers, whatever their profession of righteousness, are workers of iniquity. In Matthew 7:15 the Lord referred to the same general class of people as wolves in sheep's clothing. They deceive, mislead, destroy, and work havoc among those who confess Christ's precious name. Legalists profess to have greater righteousness than that produced by grace, but as Paul pointed out in 1 Corinthians 15:56, the law proves to be simply "the strength of sin."

"Beware of the concision," wrote the apostle. "The concision" is a contemptuous term Paul used to refer to those mutilators of the body who taught that the observance of circumcision was imperative to give one a full standing before God. The apostle would not agree that the mere ordinance is true circumcision. Since the cross, the only true circumcision is not a carnal ordinance, but the putting off of the sins of the flesh. Circumcision of the heart is recognition of the fact that the flesh has been put to death in the cross of Christ. Only as the soul accepts this and uses the sharp knife of self-judgment on his flesh is he delivered from its power.

Externalists, including legalists and ritualists of all descriptions, always make more of ordinances and outward forms than of the soul's condition and the spiritual truths symbolized by those rituals. Legalistic Israelites, who provide the best example, boasted of their connection with the temple of the Lord and gloried in legal observances while they were actually far from God and under His disapproval. Christians should not forget that it is just as possible for believers today to be occupied with ordinances and church position and to forget the more important issues of true piety and self-judgment. Nothing that God has commanded is unimportant. But our Lord said to the Jews of His time concerning their intense regard for religious rites and their neglect of justice and mercy, "These ought ye to have done, and not to leave the other undone" (Matthew 23:23).

Philippians 3:3 makes four distinct statements that we will consider in detail. The first statement is "We are the circumcision." That is, we are those who have accepted by faith the death of the flesh in the cross of Christ. We recognize the utter corruption of the flesh and its powerlessness for service to God even when placed under the most careful training and supervision. Therefore we have put off the flesh in the cross of Christ, "where there is neither Greek nor Jew, circumcision nor uncircumcision, Barbarian, Scythian, bond nor free: but Christ is all, and in all" (Colossians 3:11). We began with God by accepting the mark of judgment on the flesh; now we do not look for anything good in it, but triumph only in Christ.

The second statement in Philippians 3:3 is "We...worship God in the spirit." The worship of the old dispensation was of a ritualistic character, but the Lord Jesus told the Samaritan woman, "The hour cometh, and now is, when the true worshippers shall worship the Father in spirit and in truth" (John 4:23). Outward forms and services, music and genuflections, do not constitute worship. They may even be hindrances to it. Real worship is that of the heart. The Spirit of God shows us the things of Christ and as we are occupied with Him, true praise and adoration ascend to the Father.

The third statement is "We...rejoice [glory] in Christ Jesus." Our boast is in the Lord. We ourselves are utterly unprofitable, without anything to commend us to Him who in grace has saved us. All our boasting is about His lovingkindness and His mighty power that is exercised in mercy on our behalf.

The last statement in Philippians 3:3 is "We...have no confidence in the flesh." The flesh of the believer is no more to be trusted than the flesh of the vilest sinner. Regeneration is not a changing of flesh into spirit; nor is sanctification a gradual process of such a change within us. "That which is born of the flesh is flesh; and that which is born of the Spirit is spirit" (John 3:6). The fleshly nature is never improved, and the new nature received at the moment of new birth does not require improvement. "The carnal mind...is not subject to the law of God, neither indeed can be" (Romans 8:7). The spiritual mind is the mind of Christ. As we walk in the Spirit, we are delivered from the desires of the flesh. Even after years of godly living, the flesh itself is not the least bit better than it was at the very beginning of our Christian life. For this reason we dare not trust the flesh, for however blessed the work of God is in our souls, in our flesh "dwelleth no good thing" (Romans 7:18).

Gain and Loss (Philippians 3:4-7)

Paul had learned by experience the utter unprofitableness of the flesh. From a human standpoint, he had far more to glory in before he was converted to Christ than any of the "concision" among the Philippians had even afterward. If anyone had grounds for confidence in the flesh, or thought he had, Paul could say, "I more" (Philippians 3:4). Those to whom he wrote were Gentiles by natural birth and therefore "aliens from the commonwealth of Israel, and strangers from the covenants of promise, having no hope, and without God in the world" (Ephesians 2:12).

But it was otherwise with the apostle. He was born within the circle of the covenant. He bore in his body the mark that indicated he was within the sphere of the Abrahamic promise. Circumcised on the eighth day, he was thus separated from the Gentile world. Nor were his parents merely "proselytes of the gate"—that is, Gentiles who had forsaken idolatry and, turning to the God of Abraham,

Isaac, and Jacob, had come within the blessings of the covenant through the rite of circumcision. No, Paul was of the stock of Israel. For generations his family had belonged to the covenant people. Then too he was descended not from a bondwoman, but from the favorite wife of Jacob.

Moreover, when the ten tribes revolted and turned away from the house of David, Paul's tribe (Benjamin) had remained loyal to the true kingly line. The tribe of Benjamin had failed so grievously in the day of the judges that they were almost exterminated. But afterward, through enabling grace, they remained steadfast and thus won for themselves an immortal name. To be a Benjamite was something in which the flesh might well pride itself.

Paul could also have had "confidence in the flesh" because of his religious convictions. Saul of Tarsus had been a Hebrew of the Hebrews. He was not merely a Jew by birth, as are some who are indifferent to their Hebrew faith. To the very core of his being he was a follower of the first Hebrew, Abraham himself.

As far as the law was concerned, Paul was in practice, faith, and name a Pharisee. Of the various Jewish sects existing in his day, the Pharisees were the most intensely orthodox. They clung most tenaciously not only to the revealed Word of God, but also to a vast body of human traditions that had been handed down from their forefathers and had become in their eyes as sacred as the written Word itself. Our Lord described many of them as hypocrites, but when He wished to emphasize the need for positive righteousness, He said, "Except your righteousness shall exceed the righteousness of the scribes and Pharisees, ye shall in no case enter into the kingdom of heaven" (Matthew 5:20). He would not have referred to the Pharisees thus if it were not well known that they insisted on obedience to the law of God. On another occasion Paul said, "After the most straitest sect of our religion I lived a Pharisee" (Acts 26:5). He professed Judaism of the strictest kind, and he lived what he professed.

Paul's zeal for the traditions of the elders was seen in the fact that he was a relentless persecutor of the newborn Christians. "Exceedingly mad against them," as he himself confessed, he "persecuted them even unto strange cities" and "compelled them to blaspheme" (Acts 26:11). Yet there is no evidence that he was naturally a man of fierce and implacable disposition. In fact the words of the glorified Lord seem to imply the contrary: "It is hard for thee to kick against the pricks" (Acts 26:14). What he did, he did from a stern sense of duty, not as the fulfillment of his natural desires.

In fulfilling the righteousness that the law demanded, Paul was outwardly blameless. He told us in Romans 7 that of all the commandments there was only one that really convicted him of sin. There was no external way of detecting the violation of that one commandment; those who looked at the stalwart champion of Jewish orthodoxy could not see the covetousness that was in his heart. His outward life gave no evidence of his sin, so he could speak of himself as "blameless" (Philippians 3:6).

But then this religious bigot—this stern, unyielding champion of what he believed to be the truth of God—was brought into contact with the glorified Christ. On that never-to-be-forgotten day on the Damascus turnpike, Paul realized in one moment that "all our righteousnesses are as filthy rags" (Isaiah 64:6). "What things were gain" to him—those things on which he had been building his hopes for eternity, those things which gave him a standing in the eyes of his fellow men and caused them to look on him with admiration— he now saw in their true light. He saw all those things as utterly worthless and polluted garments, unfit to cover him before the eyes of a holy God and deserving only to be cast away. So Paul exclaimed, "What things were gain to me, those I counted loss for Christ" (Philippians 3:7).

Note that he did not count them "loss" merely for Christianity. In other words, he was not simply exchanging one religion for another; he was not replacing one system of rites and ceremonies with a superior system; he was not setting aside one set of doctrines, rules, and regulations in order to make way for a better set. Many people think that "changing their religion" is all that *conversion* means, all that God requires of them.

Paul's experience was otherwise. He came into actual contact with a divine person, the once crucified but now glorified Christ of God. He was won by that person forever, and for His sake he counted all else as loss. If anyone does not comprehend the difference between Paul's conversion and "changing religions," he is missing entirely the point the apostle was emphasizing in Philippians 3:4-7. Christ, and Christ alone, meets every need of the soul. His work has satisfied God, and it satisfies the one who trusts in Him. When we rest in Christ, our confidence in the flesh is forever ended. All our confidence is in Him who died and rose again, and who lives to intercede for us.

The Steadfast Mind (Philippians 3:8-11)

Many years of faithful witness-bearing intervened between verse 7, which closed the last section, and verse 8, which opens this. Paul had counted all things but loss for Christ when he first saw His glory on the road to Damascus, and the long and arduous years since had not lessened his devotion. He still counted all things to be of no worth compared with that which had so dazzled the vision of his soul: the excellency of the knowledge of Christ Jesus the Lord.

How different is the experience of many others. At first their love is fervent and self-sacrificing, but soon the fine gold of their devotedness dims and their early freshness passes away. When their hearts begin to "wax wanton against Christ" (1 Timothy 5:11), the world, which once seemed so worthless in view of the matchless glory shining in the face of the Savior, begins again to exercise attractive power. But never for one moment did Paul go back on the great renunciation he had made when he was won for the exalted Christ whom he had ignorantly persecuted.

And so in Philippians 3:8-11 Paul reaffirmed the faith with which he had begun. He still counted all that the world could offer as dross and refuse compared with Christ's surpassing glory, which was the focus of his life. Paul's words were not mere mystical rhapsodizing, for already he had "suffered the loss of all things," even his liberty. All his losses were in accord with the dominant purpose of his life: to "win Christ" and to "be found in him" in the great consummation (Philippians 3:8-9).

When Paul declared that he wanted to be found in Christ, he was sharing with his readers the secret of the supreme emotion of his being. The apostle was not talking about an attainment or something he hoped to earn by self-abnegation. It was as if he were saying, "Ever since I saw Christ in the glory of God, I have considered nothing else worth living for. He has so won my heart that nothing now counts with me but the blessedness of knowing Him and of being completely identified with Him in life, in death, and beyond death. Now, even if I could, I would not want to stand before God in my own righteousness. I desire only to be found in Him. I long only to know Him more intimately—let the suffering involved be what it may. I would even die as He died, or die any other way that He might choose, in order to be included in the great rapture of all saints at His coming. I want to follow whatever way will lead me to the glorious 'out-resurrection from among the dead' (literal translation of Philippians 3:11). Then I will have attained my goal. I will be so completely identified with Him who has won my heart that I will be like Him forever and with Him through all the ages to come."

This paraphrase of Paul's words shows that there is no element of uncertainty. The apostle did not fear that he might miss the first resurrection through unfaithfulness or lack of watchfulness. Those who teach that the rapture is only for certain devoted saints and that even Paul himself was haunted with the fear that he would fall short of it, lose entirely the sense of the rich grace of God. This grace will work in us that glorious change which will make us like Him for whom we wait. The consistent teaching of the apostle is that "they that are Christ's" will rise "at his coming" (1 Corinthians 15:23). In this hope the aged prisoner of the Lord faced the prospect of martyrdom in its most cruel form. Martyrdom would be merely the appointed means by which he would attain the blessedness of the first resurrection.

When Paul wrote about the out-resurrection (or resurrection out from among the dead), he was not referring to a present experience, as the verses following Philippians 3:11 show. He was referring to that one great event for which every instructed Christian should wait with eagerness: the coming of the Lord Jesus Christ and our gathering together to Him. The apostle did not have in mind the power of resurrection life working in him here on earth, enabling him to live in a "first-resurrection experience," as some have designated it. Their interpretation is dangerously near to the "death to nature" theories, which were promulgated by earnest but misled men in the last century and resulted in grave departures from sobriety and Scriptural order.

No one had more fully experienced "the power of his resurrection" (Philippians 3:10) in his human body than the apostle. Yet he thought of participation in the out-resurrection as the climax of all his years of devoted service. Everything would be incomplete without that. I know of no place in the Word of God where the expression "out-resurrection" is used in reference to the believer's present experience. In fact the prepositions in Philippians 3:11 intensify the thought of a selective resurrection; that is, Paul was referring to the first resurrection as distinguished from the second which brings up the unsaved dead for judgment (Revelation 20:4-5).

Scripture clearly teaches that there are two resurrections, not one general rising of the saved and the unsaved at the same time. "The resurrection of the just," "the resurrection of life," "the first resurrection," "the resurrection from the dead," and "the resurrection out of the dead" are all terms synonymous with the one the apostle used in Philippians 3:11. For a further explanation see "The Two Resurrections" and "The Judgment" on pages 881-888 of *The Mackintosh Treasury* by C. H. Mackintosh (Neptune, NJ: Loizeaux, 1976).

With his eye and heart set on the out-resurrection, the apostle could cast aside all obstacles that would cause him to glory in the flesh or give others occasion to glory on his behalf. Like a racer stripped of heavy garments that would impede his performance in the contest, Paul struggled ardently on, with his eye on the goal. While looking toward the out-resurrection, he could not be daunted by suffering or terrorized by death. He saw in both an opportunity for fuller, sweeter fellowship with his Lord. Paul would "count it all joy" (James 1:2) to drink of His cup of suffering and to share in His baptism of death. Of course, his share in the baptism of death was only as witness-bearer, as was promised to James and John before him (Mark 10:39).

How little most of us enter into this holy "fellowship of his sufferings" (Philippians 3:10). Some who make the greatest pretense
about fellowship in ecclesiastical things would be found sadly want-
ing if opportunity were given for them to enter into this fellowship
of sorrow and pain. In no other phase of fellowship does the soul
enter as fully into communion with Him who was on earth "a man
of sorrows, and acquainted with grief" (Isaiah 53:3).

Resurrection-Perfectness (Philippians 3:12-16)

Very early in the history of the church, there were men who con-
fused certain spiritual experiences, real or imagined, with the teaching of the Lord and His apostles in regard to the first resurrection.
Hymenaeus and Philetus, for example, are mentioned in Paul's second letter to Timothy. The apostle indicated that they had erred
concerning the truth and overthrew the faith of some by "saying
that the resurrection is past already" (2 Timothy 2:18).

Nothing is more detrimental to Christian testimony than making
lofty claims that cannot be substantiated by experience. For example
some claim that sinlessness or the eradication of the evil nature is
the privilege of Christians. If practical experience later proves to
them that it is impossible to maintain such a state, they are in grave
danger of becoming utterly disheartened and possibly renouncing
the faith entirely unless preserved by divine grace.

In Philippians 3:12-16 the apostle was careful to make it clear
that he did not claim to have reached a state of resurrection-
perfectness here on earth. To describe that state he used a word that
means "completeness" or "that to which nothing can be added."
Paul declared that he had not yet attained this state. But he did have
it in view, for he knew that at the coming of the Lord Jesus Christ
he would be made like Himself and thus forever free from all ten-
dency to sin. Meanwhile he could only "follow after," earnestly
seeking to lay hold of that for which Christ Jesus had laid hold of
him (Philippians 3:12). He could exemplify in a devoted life the
power of Christ's resurrection in which he shared.

Philippians 3:13-14 can be rendered, "Brethren, I count not

myself to have apprehended; but this one thing, forgetting those things which are behind and reaching forth unto those things which are before, I press toward the mark for the prize of the calling of God on high in Christ Jesus." Paul was professing to have apprehended, or laid hold of, only one thing. The "one thing" was the understanding that the path of blessing is found in forgetting the things that are past and seeking to lay hold of his portion in Christ from day to day while always keeping the goal in view. To do this is to "follow...holiness, without which no man shall see the Lord" (Hebrews 12:14).

It is a great mistake to teach that this verse in Hebrews means that unless one attains to certain experiences in holy living, he will be forever barred from a sight of the Lord. What the verse means is that he who will see the Lord is one who follows that which characterized his Master here: an inward and outward separation from all that is contrary to the mind of God.

The calling of God on high (Philippians 3:14) is that heavenly calling which is characteristic of the present dispensation of grace. Christ is no longer on earth and His world-kingdom has not yet been set up. But believers are linked with Him as the glorified Man at God's right hand, and they are called to represent Him on earth. The prize is the reward He will confer at the end of the race. Toward that end Paul was pressing on, counting as refuse all that would hinder his progress.

To his fellow believers the apostle said, "Let us therefore, as many as be perfect, be thus minded" (Philippians 3:15). Earlier he said that he was not perfect. Here he wrote as though he were, and linked others with him in this perfection. Was Paul contradicting himself?

The fact is that in verse 12 Paul used a word that implies perfection in growth or development. An apple in June may be a perfect apple so far, but it will have a much greater perfection or completeness in August or September. The same is true of the believer.

In verse 15 Paul used a word that refers to the perfection of full growth (somewhat like the maturity of the fathers in 1 John 2). Christians who are perfect in this sense have shunned the world and its follies. Christ has become to them the one object before the soul.

To live for Him and to seek His glory are the only things that count in their estimation.

And yet such saints are still surrounded by infirmity. They are likely to err in judgment. They may make grave mistakes and come to wrong conclusions (influenced as we all are by early education, environment, and mental capacity). They may even be misled as to doctrinal questions. Nevertheless theirs is the mind of Christ, and they may be comforted by the apostle's words in Philippians 3:15: "If in any thing ye be otherwise minded, God shall reveal even this unto you." Where there is willingness to be taught of God, the illuminating grace of the Holy Spirit can be depended on to open up His Word and to guide into all truth.

But he would be a bold man indeed who would dare to say, "I understand all truth; all mysteries are clear to me. I have perfect apprehension of divine revelation." Only the most shameless egotism could lead anyone to make such a statement. How patient we need to be with one another, how ready to confess that we know only in part. We must recognize the fact that we are always in need of further instruction.

However, there are truths and principles so plainly put in God's Word that any Spirit-taught believer may see them readily. It is our responsibility to walk in these plain truths, and we should walk in them together. As Paul said in Philippians 3:16, "Let us walk by the same rule, let us mind the same thing." We should walk together as far as possible, counting on God to reveal to us whatever may be lacking as we patiently and prayerfully learn from Him through His Word. A wider recognition of Paul's words would lead to more kindly consideration of one another and would tend to make us helpers of each other's faith rather than judges of each other's doubtful thoughts.

Enemies of the Cross (Philippians 3:17-19)

If we think of this passage as one sentence, we realize that the sentence is incomplete and needs the verses that follow it to conclude it. But I have left out the conclusion on purpose so that we may consider the first portion more carefully. The conclusion has to do with another, happier theme. In the first portion the apostle spoke of the responsibilities and snares of the pilgrim path. In the conclusion he pointed to the goal where all danger will be forever past—as will all opportunity to bear faithful testimony to a rejected Lord.

It behooves us to consider the brevity of the time allotted to us for bearing witness. It will soon be forever too late to suffer for and with Christ. It will also be too late to win an honored place in the everlasting kingdom of our Savior-God. That which we call "time" is the training school for the ages to come. It is a mistake to waste its precious moments—few at the most when compared with the eternal ages—on things that are of no lasting value.

Paul was an example both in life and doctrine for all who would come after him. It was not proud egotism that led him to plead with saints to follow him and his faithful companions as they in turn followed Christ. Paul lived what he taught. He was not one man on the platform and another in private or in business life.

We need to remember that Paul was no gentleman of leisure. He was not a clergyman afraid to soil his hands with honest labor. He worked night and day making tents when funds were low or when he felt the need of setting an example of activity to any inclined to slothfulness. Yet all the while he preached and taught publicly and from house to house with a diligence that few if any have equaled and none have surpassed. He was also careful about his personal communion with the Lord and strove to keep his conscience void of offense toward both God and man. What an example for us all to follow!

It goes without saying that he could not please everyone, even his own brethren, at all times. His work was belittled, his appearance ridiculed, his apostleship denied, and his integrity questioned. Some even intimated that he was a crafty deceiver who, by an appearance of frankness, caught the unwary with guile, and at times did evil so that good might result. Paul indignantly refuted all these charges and insinuations, but never allowed slander to embitter him. He did not return railing for railing or seek to injure those who would have injured him so willingly.

Paul kept on the even tenor of his way, living Christ and preaching Christ with unchanged ardor to the very end. His wondrous life stood as an abiding answer to those who wanted to malign him. Therefore he could say, "Be followers together of me" (Philippians 3:17). He could call on the saints to observe his consistent ways and walk in the same paths.

Centuries have rolled by since wicked men sought to dishonor Paul and since the Roman executioner's ax severed his head from his body. Long ago Paul finished his testimony in laying down his life for his Master's sake, but he still remains the pre-eminent example of what the Christian should be. Sustained by divine grace, we can pass through this valley of death's shadow as Paul did.

Let us examine our own ways and see how they measure up to his. We cannot excuse ourselves for failure on the basis of the fact that times and conditions have changed. The same One who worked so effectually in him centuries ago will work in us today if He finds a willing mind and a sanctified determination to take Paul's path of unworldliness and devotion to Christ.

Philippians 3:18-19 warn us about people who are altogether different from Paul. Many, then as now, professed to be on the pilgrim path, but their profession was hollow. They proclaimed themselves to be Christians, but their actions proved that they were "enemies of the cross of Christ." Paul did not say they were enemies of the blood or of the death of Christ; their opposition was directed against His cross, which signified His shame and rejection by the world. Paul, on the other hand, gloried in that cross. By it he saw himself crucified to the world and the world to him. But world-lovers refused to see themselves this way. They wanted the benefits of Christ's death while refusing to identify with His shame. They lived for self-indulgence, yet made a pretense of piety. The expression "whose God is their belly" really indicates that they worshiped themselves. "Belly" refers to self-gratification.

How many today live for self! But when that self is devoted to Christ, out of it flows living water for the refreshment and blessing of others (see our Lord's words in John 7:38). Until self is displaced as the object for which to live and is surrendered to God as an instrument to be used by and for Christ, there can be no true pilgrim character.

The apostle declared that for the enemies of the cross the end will be destruction. Consider the solemnity of his statement. Those who live for self-gratification while on earth will, in the life to come, be in a condition where gratification of the smallest desire will be utterly impossible. Our Lord told of one who on earth "was clothed in purple and fine linen, and fared sumptuously every day" (Luke 16:19). But when the rude hand of death suddenly snatched him away, he found himself in great torment in a place where not even his anguished prayer for a drop of water to cool his parched tongue could be granted. Such is the destruction awaiting those who live for self, ignoring the claims of the Christ of God.

Heedless of their eternal destiny, these enemies of the cross go on in their folly, indifferent to the admonitions of Scripture, conscience, and the Holy Spirit. They are also indifferent to the warnings and entreaties of men of God who, like Paul, have chosen the better part and know whereof they speak. Casting all godly counsel and sound advice to the winds, these flamboyant fools sport on the edge of a moral precipice, display their heedlessness and folly before everyone, glory in their shame, and exult in that which should cause them to bow in penitent grief before redeeming mercy.

Those who live for self are unlike Mary who chose "that good part, which shall not be taken away from her" (Luke 10:42). They are unlike Moses who chose to "suffer affliction with the people of God" rather than "enjoy the pleasures of sin for a season" (Hebrews 11:25). Instead they deliberately reject the good and choose the evil. They forfeit the hope of Heaven for a brief time of sensual or sensuous pleasure here on earth.

Paul summed up their attitude in four little words: "who mind earthly things" (Philippians 3:19). Despising the heavenly calling, they choose the earthly and become indeed "dwellers on the earth" (Isaiah 18:3), only to be exposed to the fierce wrath of God in the day when He arises to shake the earth. No wonder the apostle wept as he wrote of the enemies of the cross and warned them of their peril in pursuing their evil ways.

Heavenly Citizenship (Philippians 3:20-21)

The Greek word *politeuma* is translated "conversation" in Philippians 3:20. It means "commonwealth or citizenship" and might be transliterated "politics"; actually the word involves all three thoughts. Comprehension of its scope, as used by the apostle here, should help the Christian to understand his true relationship to and position in the affairs of this life on earth.

When Paul was writing this letter, Philippi was a Roman colony. Roman citizenship had been granted as a mark of special favor to all the free-born citizens of the former Macedonian capital. Citizenship was considered a great privilege. It enabled each Philippian, though dwelling in Macedonia, to say proudly, "My citizenship is in Rome." He was responsible to the emperor, not to the provincial government of Macedonia.

These thoughts about citizenship can be applied to the Christian. Saved by matchless grace, though still living in the world, his commonwealth—the government to which he owes primary allegiance—is in Heaven. He is subject directly to the Lord Jesus Christ, and his conduct is to be regulated by His Word.

The realization of his heavenly citizenship, while keeping the Christian free from entangling alliances with the affairs of this world, will not result in lawlessness or lack of subjection to rulers in this world. A Philippian subject to imperial authority would not be a lawbreaker in Macedonia, for it was the imperial authority that had instituted the government of Macedonia. And as the apostle told us in Romans 13:1, "The powers that be are ordained of God." Thus Paul commanded Christians to recognize the divine authority by which magistrates rule and to be subject to them in all things.

But one will search in vain the distinctly Christian part of the Bible (namely, the New Testament Epistles) for any hint that Christians are to seek worldly power or dominion during this present age. Our place is one of subjection, not rule, until Christ returns to reign.

The emperor to whom the Philippians owed allegiance lived in Rome. If he appeared in Philippi, he would recognize with special honor those whose citizenship was directly linked with the capital of the empire. Similarly our Lord is in Heaven and from there we expect Him soon to descend; then He will openly acknowledge all those whose citizenship is in Heaven. He will recognize them before an astonished and fearful world (see 2 Thessalonians 1:3-12).

As a result of archeological discoveries we know that the term *kurios,* which is the general word for "Lord" in the New Testament, was an imperial title. *Kurios* was never used in reference to an emperor until he was deified in a public pagan ceremony; thus we know that the term was used as a divine title. At the time Paul wrote his letter to the Philippians, it was common to address the brutal man who occupied the imperial throne as "our Lord Nero." How marked was the contrast when Christians, often writhing beneath the bitter persecutions of this unspeakably wicked tyrant, looked expectantly toward the heavens for the return of "our Lord Jesus Christ."

At His coming, the first resurrection will take place; the sleeping saints will be raised and living saints will be changed. First Corinthians 15:53 tells us, "This corruptible must put on incorruption, and this mortal must put on immortality." Our natural bodies will be changed to spiritual bodies.

Philippians 3:21 says that the Lord will "change our vile body." When the King James version of our Bible was translated in the seventeenth century, the word "vile" did not necessarily have the connotation of evil. That which was "vile" was lowly or common; so here "our vile body" is really the body of our humiliation—the body that links us to the lower creation, a body common to both saint and sinner. At the Lord's return it will be transformed and made like the body of His glory. In that resurrection body He came forth from the tomb, showed Himself to His disciples, ascended into Heaven, and appeared to Saul of Tarsus. In it He will soon return with glory.

The natural body is really a body suited to the soul. A spiritual body is a body suited to the spirit. It is not that one is material and the other immaterial. Both are material, although the spiritual body is of finer substance than the mortal body and no longer subject to certain laws by which the natural body is controlled.

In bodies of glory we will dwell forever in the city to which we belong even now. It is our own, our native country. As children of God we will never really be at home until we are there with our glorified Lord.

The same divine energy that worked in Christ to raise Him from the dead, will continue to work through Him until He subdues all things to Himself. Then, as we learn from 1 Corinthians 15:24-28, He will deliver the kingdom to the Father so that God in all His fullness—Father, Son, and Holy Spirit—may be "all in all" forever, fully manifested in Christ Jesus, who remains eternally our Lord and our Head.

CHAPTER FOUR

CHRIST, THE BELIEVER'S STRENGTH

Steadfastness and Unity (Philippians 4:1-3)

Having concluded the long parenthesis of chapter 3, the apostle again exhorted believers to strive for steadfastness and unity. It is evident that there was incipient division in the assembly of believers at Philippi. The Epistle to the Philippians was written in order to deal with this problem, but Paul did not put his finger on the difficulty immediately. The ministry of chapters 1–3 was an attempt to prepare the hearts of the offenders for a final word of exhortation. Then in chapter 4 he called them by name and pleaded with them not to let self-interest hinder the work of the Lord.

With expressions of deepest affection he addressed the assembly as a whole. They were his dearly beloved brethren, for whom he yearned. They would be his "joy and crown" at the judgment seat of Christ. Notice that this expression in Philippians 4:1 is analogous to that of 1 Thessalonians 2:19-20. There, addressing the saints who had been won to Christ through his ministry, he could say, "For what is our hope, or joy, or crown of rejoicing? Are not even ye in the presence of our Lord Jesus Christ at his coming? For ye are our glory and joy."

Paul was saying that when he stands at the judgment seat of Christ as His servant, that which will fill his heart with gladness will be the sight of those for whose eternal blessing he labored on earth.

Rutherford beautifully expressed the same thought when, speaking of the town in which he had labored so long, he cried:

> Oh, if one soul from Anwoth
> Meet me at God's right hand,
> My heaven will be two heavens,
> In Immanuel's land.

At the judgment seat of Christ, he who sows and he who reaps will rejoice together. Each servant will come bringing in his sheaves and, looking up into the face of the Lord, will be able to say, "Behold I and the children which God hath given me" (Hebrews 2:13).

The crown of rejoicing is the soul-winner's garland composed of those he has won for Christ. (A Christian must always stand in a more precious relationship to the one who was used for his conversion than to any other.) Those the soul-winner has won are his children in the faith, his sons and daughters in Christ Jesus. Their happy progress in the Christian life gladdens his heart and is rich reward for his service on their behalf. On the other hand, their failure—as evidenced by loss of interest in divine things, by dissension, or by resumption of worldly ways—must rend his heart with grief and fill him with a sense of shame.

"Now we live," wrote Paul in 1 Thessalonians 3:8, "if ye stand fast in the Lord." A brother-servant, the apostle John, wrote to his converts, "And now, little children, abide in him; that, when he shall appear, we may have confidence, and not be ashamed before him at his coming" (1 John 2:28). Notice that John said "that...*we*...may not be ashamed" (italics added), not *they*. He was not referring to the shame of converts who failed, but to the shame of those who were instrumental in leading them to Christ.

So Paul earnestly exhorted his beloved Philippians to "stand fast" in the faith. Satan is always trying to hinder the people of God from clinging steadfastly together and presenting a united front to the enemy. It is unfortunate that his efforts to introduce dissension so readily succeed because of the flesh.

In Philippians 4:2, without further delay and with perfect frankness, the apostle spoke directly to the two offenders against unity (whom he had in mind from the beginning of the letter). There is no sternness, no lording it over their consciences; instead there is pleading. As though Christ Himself were beseeching, Paul entreated Euodias and Syntyche. They had been earnest laborers in the gospel, but they had quarreled, so Paul exhorted them to "be of the same mind in the Lord."

Paul certainly did not mean by that they had to think alike in everything or see all things from the same standpoint. That would have been asking for the impossible. The very possession of mind, which distinguishes men from animals, gives occasion for differences of judgment and so calls for much patience. No two people ever see the same rainbow. The slightest difference of position gives each a view at a different angle. The formation and contour of the eye also affect the view. One person may be able to discern every distinct shade while another person may be colorblind. No amount of argument or persuasion will enable the second person to see what is so clear to the first.

We might even say that no two people have ever read the same Bible. Of course there is not one book from God for one person and a different book for another, but there is a difference in our understanding. We are so influenced by our environment and our education that we are prejudiced without realizing it. Even when we try to be open-minded, we are often misled by our impressions and the limitations of our comprehension. Therefore we need to be patient with each other.

But if what we have been saying is true, how can we be of one mind? Philippians 4:2 makes the answer plain, for Paul beseeched Euodias and Syntyche to "be of the same mind *in the Lord*" (italics added). If both had the lowly mind of Christ, if both sought to be subject to the Lord even though there were differences of judgment, each would respect the other's viewpoint and neither would try to control the other's conscience. Then there would be no reason for dissension.

Unfortunately we do not always have the lowly mind and often we insist on what seems to be an exceedingly important truth when nothing vital is at stake. An equally honest and earnest brother or sister in Christ may fail to see things as we see them. At the judgment seat of Christ, it may be revealed that they, not we, were right—or perhaps that both of us were wrong.

Philippians 4:3 was probably spoken by Paul directly to Epaphroditus, to whom the apostle was, I presume, dictating this letter. Epaphroditus, having fulfilled his mission and having regained strength after his illness, was about to return to Philippi and he was to be the bearer of this Epistle. The apostle entreated him as a true yokefellow to help Euodias and Syntyche reach the unity of mind about which he had been writing.

Paul mentioned that the two women had labored "in the gospel" with him, with Clement, and with others whose names, though not given here, are in the book of life. We are not to understand from Paul's words that the women had occupied the public platform, taught in the assembly of God's people, or participated in public testimony, for this would contradict the words of the Holy Ghost given through Paul in 1 Corinthians 14:33-34 and 1 Timothy 2:9-15.

There are many Scriptural ways in which devoted women can serve the Lord "in the gospel." In oriental as well as occidental lands, the gospel work done by women is of tremendous importance. Godly women may have free access to many places where men cannot go. Laboring "in the gospel" implies a great deal more than simply speaking from a platform. In many instances speaking from a platform may be of lesser value than individual heart-to-heart work.

Epaphroditus evidently caught the note of inspiration in Paul's personal words to him, and so he included them in the Epistle. We can be thankful to God that these words have come down to us. They give us deeper insight into the working of the spirit of grace in the mind of Paul, and until the church's history on earth has ended, these words will be valuable to all who seek to serve the Lord.

Joy and Confidence (Philippians 4:4-7)

In Philippians 3:1 Paul wrote, "Finally, my brethren, rejoice in the Lord." Undoubtedly, as far as his own mind was concerned, the apostle was ready to bring his letter to a close. But, as we have already seen, this was not the mind of the Spirit. Like his brother-apostle Jude, Paul was led to exhort the saints to "earnestly contend for the faith which was once delivered" (Jude 3).

Now in Philippians 4:4 Paul again referred to that which was so much on his heart: he exhorted the saints to "rejoice in the Lord." Joy and holiness are inseparable. Holy Christians are able to rejoice even when passing through the deepest afflictions. But believers who through lack of watchfulness have permitted themselves to fall into unholy ways, lose immediately the joy of the Lord, which is the strength of those who walk in communion with Christ.

A second exhortation (see Philippians 4:5) is one we should earnestly heed: "Let your moderation be known unto all men." Moderation is a most commendable Christian virtue, but the word translated "moderation" has other meanings. The word has been rendered "yieldingness" by some. This translation is excellent and suggests that Paul is urging resilience of character, which many of us sadly lack. Rotherham translated the word as "considerateness" and the Revised Version renders it as "forbearance" or "gentleness." All these various meanings are summed up, I think, in Matthew Arnold's rendering. This English critic translated the passage, "Let your sweet reasonableness be manifested to all men." He pointed out the interesting fact that the original word is unknown in classical Greek; it was his impression that Paul coined the word for the occasion.

Sweet reasonableness is a lovely trait in a Christian. It is the very opposite of that unyielding, harshly dogmatic, self-determined spirit which so often dominates in place of the meekness and gentleness of Christ. "I beseech you, my brethren," wrote Cromwell to the warring theologians of his day, "remember that it is possible you *may* be wrong." We are apt to forget this when we are engaged in discussions about doctrines, methods of service, or church principles.

Sweet reasonableness does not indicate a lack in intensity of conviction or a lack of assurance about the correctness of doctrines, principles, or practices that one believes he has learned from the Word of God. But it does imply a kindly consideration for the judgment of others who may be equally sincere and equally devoted—and possibly even more enlightened. Nothing is ever lost by recognizing this and by remembering that we all know only "in part" (1 Corinthians 13:12).

How apt is the brief sentence that follows the exhortation to sweet reasonableness: "The Lord is at hand." I take it that the thought here is not exactly that the Lord is coming; rather it is that the Lord is standing by, looking on, hearing every word spoken, taking note of every action. "Closer is He than breathing, / Nearer than hands or feet." If believers truly realized that He is "at hand," strife and dissension would quickly cease and the forbearance and grace exhibited in Christ would be seen in His followers.

In Philippians 4:6 a wonderful promise in connection with prayer is based on a third exhortation. Our Lord warned against anxious thoughts, and the Holy Spirit expanded His teaching by saying here, "Be careful [anxious] for nothing."

But how am I to obey an exhortation like this when troubles are surging around me and my restless mind will not be at peace? I need to talk to someone, but like the psalmist, "I am so agitated, that I cannot speak" (F. W. Grant's translation of Psalm 77:4). What should I do? To whom should I turn? It is natural to worry and fret in circumstances such as these, even though I tell myself over and over again that nothing is gained by worrying, and my trouble only seems to become exaggerated as I try to carry my own burdens.

The Spirit of God points the way out. He wants me to bring everything—the great things and the little things, the perplexing conditions and the trying circumstances—into the presence of God and leave them there. "By prayer and supplication," not forgetting thanksgiving for past and present mercies, He wants me to pour out my requests to God. I may feel that I do not know the mind of the Lord in regard to them, but that need not stop me. I am to make known my requests, counting on His wisdom to do for me what is best both for time and for eternity. If I cast my cares on Him and leave everything in His own blessed hands, the peace of God will guard my heart and mind through Christ Jesus. This peace is that which He Himself always enjoys, even though storms and darkness may be round about. It is a peace that passes all understanding.

I cannot obtain this peace for myself. I may tell myself over and over not to fret, but my thoughts, like untamed horses with bits in their teeth, run away with me. Or like an attacking army, worries crowd into the citadel of my mind and threaten to overwhelm me. But God, by the Holy Spirit, has promised to garrison my mind and protect my restless heart so that my thoughts will neither run away with me nor overwhelm me. Every thought will be brought into captivity to the obedience to Christ.

I will enjoy the peace of God, a peace beyond all human comprehension, as I leave my burdens where faith delights to cast every care. I leave them at the feet of Him who, having not withheld His own Son, has now declared that through Him He will freely give me all things. I can rest in this promise because He cannot deny Himself.

Holiness and Peace (Philippians 4:8-9)

Philippians 4:8-9 concludes the apostle's instructions. All that follows (verses 10-23) is a postscript of much practical value, although not addressed directly to the saints as homiletic teaching.

Throughout the Epistle, Paul presented Christ to his readers in many different aspects. Now in Philippians 4:8-9 the apostle summed his presentation up in a brief exhortation to think on holy things. He thus recognized the Old Testament principle, "As [a man] thinketh in his heart, so is he" (Proverbs 23:7).

Thinking of "these things" in an abstract way, many have missed the point Paul was making. The apostle was not just urging us to fill our minds with beautiful sentiments and poetic ideals. It would be exceedingly difficult to think on things true, honest, just, pure, and lovely without focusing on a concrete example. We have an example before us in our Lord Jesus Christ (the perfect man), in whom all these qualities are found. And to a certain degree these qualities are reproduced by the Holy Spirit in all who have been made partakers of the divine nature.

When we link Philippians 4:8-9 with 4:2, we realize that Euodias and Syntyche needed to see what the Spirit had accomplished in each other. If Euodias looked critically on Syntyche and dwelt on what was contrary to the virtues mentioned in verse 8, the breach between them would be widened immeasurably. If Syntyche retorted by exaggerating every defect or shortcoming in Euodias, she would soon become so alienated from her sister in Christ that reconciliation would be almost impossible.

If, on the other hand, Euodias and Syntyche, realized that they both had been redeemed to God by the same precious blood and were indwelt by the same Holy Spirit, they would be determined to think of each other's virtues, to recognize in each other anything worthy of praise, and to refuse to indulge in unkind criticism. As each magnified the other's graces and minimized her faults, each would be so attracted to what was of Christ in the other that she would find herself linked in heart to the one from whom she previously had turned coldly away.

Is not this kind of thinking what we all need in our dealings with one another? In every truly converted soul can be found virtues produced by the Spirit of God, evidences of the new nature: things that are honest, just, pure, lovely, and of good report. If we think on these things instead of dwelling on the failures to which we all are liable, our fellowship will become increasingly precious as the days go by. Even when there is actual cause for blame, we should stop to consider the circumstances that may have led up to that which seems so blameworthy. Then Christian pity and compassion will take the place of criticism and unkind judgment. Criticism cannot restore the erring one; it only drives him further into sin. "To err is human; to forgive divine" (Alexander Pope).

Even the secular world recognizes the folly of judging that which the eye cannot see. A Scottish poet taught us: "We only ken the wrang that's dune, / We ken na' what's resisted." We may blame a wrongdoer for things that have already deeply troubled his heart and conscience and have already been cleansed away by "the washing of water by the word" as applied by the Lord Jesus Himself (Ephesians 5:26).

Of course it is important that we never permit our minds to feed like carrion vultures on the wicked, filthy, and unholy things of the flesh, as the carnal man naturally does. The carnal mind is still present in believers, and will be until the day our bodies of humiliation are changed and made like Christ's body of glory. But we are not to allow the carnal mind to dominate us, since the Holy Spirit dwells in us to control us for Christ. There is so much that is honest, so much that is just or righteous, so much that is pure, so much that is lovely and lovable, so much that is of good report, so much that is virtuous and trustworthy, that it would be foolish for us to be occupied with their opposites.

As we meditate on things that are positive and good, we "grow in grace, and in the knowledge of our Lord and Saviour Jesus Christ" (2 Peter 3:18), for all the beautiful traits Paul mentioned were fully exemplified in Him. As noted before, they have also been imparted in measure to each of His servants—probably in larger measure to Paul than to anyone else. So without pride but as an example to the flock of Christ, the apostle could add, "Those things, which ye have both learned, and received, and heard, and seen in me, do."

As we walk the Christian path according to the power of the indwelling Spirit, we have the sweet assurance that "the God of peace shall be with you." These words of assurance connect all the exhortations in Philippians 4:8-9 with the promise of 4:7, where we are told that the peace of God will guard the minds and hearts of all who cast their cares on Him. In 4:9 we learn that the God of peace will walk with those who seek to walk before Him in piety and holiness of mind and practice.

Gratitude and Assurance (Philippians 4:10-23)

In this closing section of the Epistle, Paul thanked the assembly of believers at Philippi for the practical way in which they had demonstrated their fellowship in the gospel. They were not like those who are willing to profit eternally through the gospel ministry, but have very little concern about the temporal welfare of the servants of Christ to whom they owe the knowledge of that truth which has made them free. From the beginning of their Christian lives, the Philippian saints had cared for the needs of the apostle as opportunities arose. They even sent funds to him when he was laboring in Thessalonica, where he and his companions had gone after being released from the Philippian jail.

But years had elapsed since then and Paul had traveled far and passed through many varied experiences. Often he had found it impossible to keep in close touch with the different churches he had been used of God to establish. Consequently it was not strange that at times it seemed as if his dearest friends had forgotten him. But they had not forgotten him. The love was there, but they had lacked opportunity to display it. When the Philippians learned that he was in Rome and that he was a prisoner for the truth's sake, they hastened to show their fellowship in his sufferings by sending Epaphroditus with a gift of love.

In acknowledging their kindness, Paul took the occasion to glorify God for His care of him even when the churches had forgotten their indebtedness to him. The apostle had known cold neglect, but such indifference had never soured his spirit or led him to complain. Paul noted the coldheartedness, but he did not find fault. He left it all with the Lord and committed his circumstances to Him. Assured that He never forgot and was never an unconcerned spectator of His servant's sufferings, Paul accepted people's neglect as a lesson in the school of God. The apostle could say, "I have learned, in whatsoever state I am, therewith to be content" (Philippians 4:11).The Lord was his portion, and he could rest in the knowledge of Christ's unchanging love and care.

Paul had not in a moment learned to be content. Like all disciples in God's school, he had to advance in the life of faith by learning practically the things he later taught to others. But he had earned his degree, so to speak, and he could now declare, "I know both how to be abased, and I know how to abound: every where and in all things I am instructed both to be full and to be hungry, both to abound and to suffer need" (Philippians 4:12). These are blessed lessons. The soul is never really at rest in the trials and testings of life until these precious secrets have been learned.

John Wesley is reported to have said that he did not know which dishonored God the most: to worry (which really is to doubt His love and care) or to curse and swear. Every saint would shrink from the latter with abhorrence, but many of us have no sense of the wrong we do when we worry. Our attitude should always be to rest in faith on the knowledge that "all things work together for good to them that love God, to them who are the called according to his purpose" (Romans 8:28).

Those who go forth to serve in entire dependence on the One who has sent them out as His ambassadors, are called on to exemplify the trusting attitude in a very special sense as they minister in Word and doctrine. This leads me to say something about the New Testament principle for the support of those who labor entirely in spiritual things. First let it be noted that there is no such thing in Scripture as putting the servant of God on the low level of a salary basis. In the Bible the only man hired by the year as a "minister" was the apostate Levite who was engaged by Micah of mount Ephraim and later by the Danites to be their father and priest (Judges 17–18). In the legal dispensation Jehovah was the portion of the Levites. They prospered and were cared for according to the measure in which God blessed His people and their hearts responded to His goodness. In the Christian economy we have no special clerical or extra-priestly class to be supported as professional men by their so-called lay brethren. The distinction between clergy and laity is utterly unscriptural; it is part of the Judaizing system that has perverted the truth of the church.

But there are those who are specially gifted as evangelists, pastors, and teachers, and in many instances these believers are called on to separate themselves from secular pursuits in order to devote their time exclusively to spiritual service. In the early church such men "went forth, taking nothing of the Gentiles" (3 John 7). They depended on the Lord to supply their needs and He cared for them through His own grateful people, who obeyed the injunction in Galatians 6:6: "Let him that is taught in the word communicate unto him that teacheth in all good things." Inspired by the Spirit, John wrote, "We therefore ought to receive such, that we might be fellowhelpers to the truth" (3 John 8). Such teachers have a claim on the people of God—not because they are official ministers, but because they are engaged in making known the truth. All believers are privileged to share in their service by supporting their work.

Observe carefully, however, that the servant of God is never to look to the saints for his support. He is to look directly to the Lord; he is to make his personal needs known only to Him. The servant of God should not hesitate to contact assemblies of believers to acquaint them with special opportunities for ministry to others as occasions arise. Paul did this frequently and earnestly. But rather than mention his personal needs, the apostle labored with his own hands. He did not feel he was degrading his calling by doing this. Rather, he felt that by laboring with his hands he was able to "provide things honest in the sight of all men" (Romans 12:17) and set an example to any who were inclined to seek an easy path and depend on support from those in better circumstances.

The principle is clear: The servant of Christ is to go forth in absolute dependence on the One who has commissioned him and who makes Himself responsible to meet his needs. At the same time, the people of God are called on to pray about what share they should have in the support of those who are engaged in fulltime ministry. No ministering brother has the right or authority to demand support from the saints. They, not he, must judge whether he is worthy of support. But if they benefit from his spiritual ministry, he should receive material benefits from them (see 1 Corinthians 9:11). "They which preach the gospel should live of the gospel" (1 Corinthians 9:14).

If a servant of the Lord finds fault because his support is small, he is showing that his dependence is on man rather than on God. But if the saints are callously indifferent to the temporal needs of one whom they recognize as a God-sent messenger, they show that they are out of touch with Him who has given them the privilege of helping financially in the spread of the truth. Both those who minister and those who are ministered to should seek direction from the Lord about their mutual responsibilities.

Paul had walked in dependence on the Lord for many years. As he looked back over the journey and saw how he had been sustained of God, he knew he could count on Him for the future. He faced the days to come with the assurance that he could do all things through Christ who was his strength. The One who was his life, example, and object was also his unfailing source of supply for every emergency that might arise, even a martyr's death.

While Paul did not look to man for his supplies, he was truly grateful for those who ministered to him. He did not take for granted the gift of love sent by his dear Philippian children in the faith. He expressed himself in most appreciative terms as he thanked them for their fellowship. In his expression of gratitude he is an example to all of Christ's servants, some of whom have been neglectful of courtesies that often mean more to the saints than they realize.

Paul did not receive the gift of the Philippians because he desired to profit from their generosity. He received the gift because he saw in it evidence of the working of the Spirit of grace in their souls. The Spirit was working for their blessing as well as his. And so he gladly accepted the gift, seeing in it "an odour of a sweet smell, a sacrifice acceptable, wellpleasing to God" (Philippians 4:18).

The Lord—for whose glory the Philippians ministered to His imprisoned servant—would not allow them to put Him in their debt. Instead He promised to supply all their need "according to his riches in glory by Christ Jesus" (Philippians 4:19). When we have given to our utmost limit, we have only returned a little of His own, and even that He will abundantly repay.

The last three verses of the Epistle give the concluding salutation. Note how "every saint" is again greeted affectionately (Philippians 4:21; compare 1:1); Paul refused to recognize any factions. All the believers who were with Paul joined in the salutation. He particularly mentioned those "of Caesar's household" who belonged to the imperial guard (4:22). Some of these were evidently new converts, having come to the faith as a result of their contact with Paul in his prison cell.

We close our meditations on this instructive Epistle with a message of grace ringing in our souls. "The grace of our Lord Jesus Christ be with you all. A-men" (Philippians 4:23).

AUTHOR BIOGRAPHY

HENRY ALLAN IRONSIDE, one of this century's greatest preachers, was born in Toronto, Canada, on October 14, 1876. He lived his life by faith; his needs at crucial moments were met in the most remarkable ways.

Though his classes stopped with grammar school, his fondness for reading and an incredibly retentive memory put learning to use. His scholarship was well recognized in academic circles with Wheaton College awarding an honorary Litt.D. in 1930 and Bob Jones University an honorary D.D. in 1942. Dr. Ironside was also appointed to the boards of numerous Bible institutes, seminaries, and Christian organizations.

"HAI" lived to preach and he did so widely throughout the United States and abroad. E. Schuyler English, in his biography of Ironside, revealed that during 1948, the year HAI was 72, and in spite of failing eyesight, he "gave 569 addresses, besides participating in many other ways." In his eighteen years at Chicago's Moody Memorial Church, his only pastorate, every Sunday but two had at least one profession of faith in Christ.

H. A. Ironside went to be with the Lord on January 15, 1951. Throughout his ministry, he authored expositions on 51 books of the Bible and through the great clarity of his messages led hundreds of thousands, worldwide, to a knowledge of God's Word. His words are as fresh and meaningful today as when first preached.

The official biography of Dr. Ironside, *H. A. Ironside: Ordained of the Lord*, is available from the publisher.

THE WRITTEN MINISTRY OF
H. A. IRONSIDE

Expositions

Joshua
Ezra
Nehemiah
Esther
Psalms (1-41 only)
Proverbs
Song of Solomon
Isaiah
Jeremiah
Lamentations
Ezekiel
Daniel
The Minor Prophets
Matthew
Mark
Luke
John

Acts
Romans
1 & 2 Corinthians
Galatians
Ephesians
Philippians
Colossians
1 & 2 Thessalonians
1 & 2 Timothy
Titus
Philemon
Hebrews
James
1 & 2 Peter
1,2, & 3 John
Jude
Revelation

Doctrinal Works

Baptism
Death and Afterward
Eternal Security of the Believer
Holiness: The False and
  the True
The Holy Trinity

Letters to a Roman Catholic
  Priest
The Levitical Offerings
Not Wrath But Rapture
Wrongly Dividing the Word
  of Truth

Historical Works

The Four Hundred Silent Years
A Historical Sketch of the Brethren Movement

Other works by the author are brought back into print from time to time. All of this material is available from your local Christian bookstore or from the publisher.

LOIZEAUX

A Heritage of Ministry . . .

Paul and Timothy Loizeaux began their printing and publishing activities in the farming community of Vinton, Iowa, in 1876. Their tools were rudimentary: a hand press, several fonts of loose type, ink, and a small supply of paper. There was certainly no dream of a thriving commercial enterprise. It was merely the means of supplying the literature needs for their own ministries, with the hope that the Lord would grant a wider circulation. It wasn't a business; it was a ministry.

Our Foundation Is the Word of God

We stand without embarrassment on the great fundamentals of the faith: the inspiration and authority of Scripture, the deity and spotless humanity of our Lord Jesus Christ, His atoning sacrifice and resurrection, the indwelling of the Holy Spirit, the unity of the church, the second coming of the Lord, and the eternal destinies of the saved and lost.

Our Mission Is to Help People Understand God's Word

We are not in the entertainment business. We only publish books and computer software we believe will be of genuine help to God's people, both through the faithful exposition of Scripture and practical application of its principles to contemporary need.

Faithfulness to the Word and consistency in what we publish have been hallmarks of Loizeaux through four generations. And that means when you see the name Loizeaux on the outside, you can trust what is on the inside. That is our promise to the Lord...and to you.

If Paul and Timothy were to visit us today they would still recognize the work they began in 1876. Because some very important things haven't changed at all...this is still a ministry.